JOE SAWARD

FASCINATING
FORMULA 1
FACTS

VOLUME I

JOE SAWARD

FASCINATING
FORMULA 1
FACTS

VOLUME I

First published in 2018 by Joe Saward

3 5 7 9 8 4 5 5 1

All rights reserved

Copyright © Joe Saward 2018

The right of Joe Saward to be identified as the author of this work has asserted his right under the Copyright, Designs and Patents Act 1988.

This book is in copyright. Subject to statutory exception and to provisions of relevant collective licensing agreements, no reproduction of any part may take place without the written permission of the author.

www.morienval.com

This book is sold subject to the conditions that it shall not, by way of trade or otherwise, be lent, re-sold, hired out, or otherwise circulated without the publisher's prior consent in any form of binding or cover other than that in which it is published and without a similar condition including this condition being imposed on the subsequent purchaser.

ISBN 978-0-9554868-3-8

Printed and bound in the United Kingdom by
Lightning Source
6 Precedent Drive, Rooksley,
Milton Keynes, Buckinghamshire
MK13 8PR

For my rock

How it all began...

This book was not exactly an accident, but nor was it really planned.

It just sort of happened.

The process began in the second week of December 2016. The FIA Formula 1 World Championship had ended on November 27 in Abu Dhabi, with a terrific finale between Mercedes team-mates Lewis Hamilton and Nico Rosberg. The latter had won - and promptly announced his retirement. The fans of the sport were facing a long and quiet winter, with the first race of 2017 not due until March 26, almost four months away. I decided, on a whim, that I would write a small item each day on my blog (www.joeblogsf1.com), which I hoped would be fascinating to F1 fans. The goal was to keep up interest in the sport - and traffic to the website, while at the same time allowing me to have some time off over Christmas and the New Year.

Having been around the Formula 1 "village" for 30 years, I thought it might be fun to give readers some insights into the rich history of the sport.

It began with a simple, and rather silly, fact: "In 1952 Richard Kuchen built a V8 for the AFM team. In German "kuchen" means cake – so we have had a Cake F1 engine". And it went from there...

What is a Grand Prix?

Unlikely though it might seem, the term "Grand Prix" is the fault of King Louis XIV, who ruled France between 1638 and 1715. He is best remembered for building the extravagant Château de Versailles and for his patronage of the arts, allowing literature, painting and music to flourish.

In 1648 he established the Académie Royale de Peinture et de Sculpture and 15 years later, in 1663, this organization had an idea to stimulate more artistic endeavour. Each year, it was decided, there would be a big prize offered for the best painter and the best sculptor. In French, a big prize is a "Grand Prix" and, if used in the plural, this becomes "Grands Prix". These big prizes proved to be so successful that by the 1720s other national Académies were offering their own Grands Prix for architecture, mathematics and science.

It was not really of that much interest to the man in the street but eventually the phrase slipped into sport or, more specifically, horse racing - the sport of kings.

Napoleon Bonaparte began to organize horse racing in France in 1805, with plans for horse racing events in each *département* (similar to a county) and on 11 October 1811 the winners of these competitions raced one another on a course laid out in the Champs de Mars, the gardens which today lie between the Eiffel Tower and the École Militaire. It was called the Grand Prix Impérial.

By 1863 the first Grand Prix de Paris had been inaugurated and it would quickly become the biggest event on the French equestrian calendar. Other racecourses took up the idea and Grands Prix were held in Chantilly, Deauville and at Pau, the primary city in the Béarn region, at the foot of the Pyrénées mountain range, which divides France from its neighbour Spain.

It was in Pau in 1901 that the local Automobile Club du Béarn decided to use the name for a Grand Prix du Sud-Ouest, offering several prizes for different classes: the Grand Prix de Pau was awarded to the overall winner, Maurice Farman in his Panhard; the Grand Prix du Palais d'Hiver was awarded to two drivers: Henri Farman - Maurice's brother - who won the light car class in a Darracq, and to Louis Renault, who drove the winning small car, known as a voiturette.

Even then, however, the expression Grand Prix did not really gain international recognition in the automobile world until 1906 when the Automobile Club de

France adopted the phrase for its new international event, the Grand Prix de l'ACF, held on a circuit made up of public roads, to the east of the city of Le Mans. Initially there was only one Grand Prix each year, but the use of the name gradually spread to other events, and to other countries. By the 1920s, everyone had a Grand Prix and the top class of racing became known as Grand Prix racing.

The biggest races then began to be termed a "Grande Épreuve", which means Big Test, to distinguish them from all the common or garden Grands Prix.

World War II came and went and as Europe began to rebuild, the Association Internationale des Automobile Clubs Reconnus decided (wisely) to change its name and became the Fédération Internationale de l'Automobile. It declared that there would be a new Grand Prix class called Formula A.

The first races to the new rules were held on the streets of Nice in April 1946, but the formula was not widely adopted until 1948, with a World Championship launched in 1950. Somehow, along the way, people stopped calling it Formula A and it became Formula 1. No-one is quite sure why.

How to sex an automobile

It may not suit FIA President Jean Todt's current ambitions, but the FIA, established in 1904 as the Association Internationale des Automobile Clubs Reconnus, was set up to deal with motor racing. It was a concept agreed by the representatives of the six nations taking part in the Gordon Bennett Cup race at Bad Homberg, near Frankfurt in Germany, agreed that it would be a good idea to have a federation of motor clubs to run the organisation of international motor sport. The founders were France, Germany, Italy, Great Britain, Austria and Belgium. They were soon joined by seven others (Denmark, the Netherlands, Portugal, Spain, Switzerland, the United States and Russia.

All the FIA's other roles have been added since then, but the reality is that it is still primarily known as the governing body of motorsport events.

The Formula 1 World Championship is the FIA's primary championship, and its most significant source of revenue.

The interesting thing is that the foundation of the federation came nine years after the establishment of the Automobile Club de France (ACF) and just three years after the first legal definition of an automobile. The word "automobile" was first used in France in 1861. It had its roots in Greek (autos, meaning self) and in Latin (mobilis, meaning movable). The two morphemes were stuck together to create the description "véhicule automobile". Initially this was used only for steam-powered buses.

The name was accepted by the Académie Française in 1875, although it was at that time by no means the only word used for a self-propelled vehicle, other notable names being the French expression "locomobile" or the words "motorcar' and "autocar" in English. Things became complicated as the popularity of self-propelled vehicles spread, and in 1900 the Conseil d'Etat, which advises the government on legal matters, asked the Académie Française about the word "automobile", because it was preparing a decree to regulate the new road-going vehicles. The Académie discussed the matter and decided to use what was known as Malherbe's Rule, which meant that they would follow the common usage. They then discovered that the word was regularly used in both masculine and feminine forms - and no-one knew which was correct.

They could not both be right. Foreign words did not help at all. The French word for car is "voiture", which is feminine, but is used in France for all wheeled devices, such as carts and trucks; the word "car" is masculine, but is used in France to describe a bus or coach.

In the end they decided that the only solution was to take a vote on the subject. There are 40 members of the Académie at any given moment and in 1900 this included such luminaries as the poet Sully Prudhomme, the novelist Anatole France and the Vicomte de Vogüé (father of a future FIA President). Of the 40 members only 10 turned up for the vote and seven voted for the automobile to become feminine and three voted for masculine.

Officially, the decision was taken because "voiture" is feminine, but there is a story that the some of the Académicians voted because they believed that the noisy and unreliable cars of the day were as troublesome as women...

When is an F1 driver not an F1 driver?

It is strange to relate that there is no official rule about what constitutes a Formula 1 career. In theory, one might argue that if you have driven a Formula 1 car, you can call yourself an F1 driver. Most people in the sport, however, consider an F1 driver to be someone who has qualified for, and raced in, an FIA Formula 1 World Championship Grande Épreuve.

The reason there are no rules is that no official body has ever established them. This is a great shame because sports fans are often excited by statistics and are happy to buy publications about the sport. People buy the Wisden Cricketers' Almanack or they buy books about the records in baseball. It is commercial opportunity which is being wasted.

The best F1 statistical guide was always the celebrated "Marlboro Book", an unofficial guide to F1 statistics which was published each year, sponsored by the cigarette company, and edited by the Swiss F1 journalist Jacques Deschenaux.

His records included all those who ever attempted to qualify for a Grand Prix, so the likes of Bernie Ecclestone get into the listings, but he uses the "GP Contested" measure to weed out those who did not actually start a race. If you read Wikipedia, for example, you will see that it lists the number of races entered and the number of starts, but no-one seems to agree. Alain Prost's starts numbered 199, according to Wikipedia, while Deschenaux says it was 198.

There are no set rules and so there are often disagreements and it is difficult to retro-fit any system because of all the weird things which have happened over time in F1, not least drivers crashing on the laps that are before the pre-grid and the parade lap (known as the recognition laps), such as Romain Grosjean did in Brazil in 2016.

In the days before the Safety Car was introduced there were rules which were very different to today. If a race was stopped after fewer than two full laps, for example, the race was restarted as a new event. This led to some bizarre statistics, such as Mike Thackwell, who started the 1980 Canadian GP in a third Tyrrell. The race was stopped because of a first corner accident. Thackwell's car was taken over by the senior Tyrrell driver, Jean-Pierre Jarier, who had damaged his own car in the crash. So, did Thackwell really take part in the race? Deschenaux says yes. Others say no.

It is a similar story with Jacques Laffite at the 1986 British GP, the race in which he was due to start his 177th Grand Prix, beating Graham Hill's record of 176 starts. At the start of the race poor Laffite was shoved off and crashed into a very solid wall. He broke both his legs. The race was declared null and void and so poor Jacques never started the race in which he broke his legs… and never broke the record. Deschenaux, by the way, lists Laffite as having only 174 starts.

All the rules go out of the window when one considers the German Hans Heyer, who has the unique distinction in F1 of having achieved a DNQ, DSQ and DNF all in the same event, having failed to qualify, he started the race illegally by simply driving down the pit lane and joining in. His car later broke down and was eventually disqualified – but he did race, even if officially he did not.

The longest F1 career, it seems, was that of Brazil's Rubens Barrichello, who competed in 326 Grands Prix between 1993 and 2011. The shortest F1 career, so they say, belongs to a German engineer called Ernst Loof, who qualified for only one race - the 1953 German GP - driving a Veritas. He retired with fuel pump failure just six feet ahead of his grid position. At least he got that far…

In the modern era, the Italian Marco Apicella's career (in a Jordan) lasted only as far as the first corner at Monza in the Italian Grand Prix of 1993, where he was taken out in an accident.

Some strange F1 records

Formula 1 records are a curious collection of the wonderful and bizarre, if one looks beyond the obvious most wins, most poles and so on.

A good example of this is German Markus Winkelhock, who took part in only one Grand Prix, driving a Spyker, after Christijan Albers's sponsorship failed to materialise for the 2007 European Grand Prix.

Markus was the 27-year-old son of Manfred Winkelhock, who was an F1 driver in the 1980s, before his death in a sports car crash at Mosport Park in 1985 - when Markus was five. Winkelhock Jr qualified last on the grid at the Nürburgring, but by the third lap of the race he was in the lead by more than half a minute, having been the only driver in the field to be using the right choice of tyres. The decision was a risk, but when you have nothing to lose... His moment of glory was short because the rain was so bad that the race was neutralised with a Safety Car and then red-flagged. At the restart Winkelhock was on pole, and thus became the only F1 driver ever to start at both ends of the grid for the same race. And then he lost his job to a pay-driver...

There have, in fact, been three Winkelhocks who tried to be F1 drivers, the third being Joachim, Manfred's brother and Markus's uncle, who failed to qualify an AGS in seven attempts in 1989 - in the age of pre-qualifying. He was a very decent driver, but in the wrong car, although he did go on to win Le Mans. His cv is actually pretty impressive with a German F3 title, a DTM championship, victories the in Spa and Nürburgring 24 Hour races - and a BTCC title as well. Smokin' Jo was also an Asia Pacific touring car champion.

In comparison, it is worth noting that there have been only three drivers in F1 history with the surname Hill - and all three won the World Championship, although Phil Hill was no relation to Graham and Damon.

But the weirdest of these three-of-a-kind records was at the European GP in 1997 at Jerez where the World Championship showdown qualifying resulted in the two title challengers and Heinz-Harald Frentzen, all lapping the track in 1m21.072s - having exactly the same pole lap time - to the thousandth of a second. The probability of the happening was less than tiny - and it is not likely to happen again for at least another 100 years, although perhaps some statistician out there will work out the mathematical probability.

Mind you, what is the probability of a driver achieving three pole positions in his Formula 1 career and never leading a single lap in a race? Well, that happened to Teo Fabi. He was quick, but his starts were obviously not much good - or he was just plain unlucky. I tend to go for the latter explanation as there was one occasion when his Benetton team-mate, Gerhard Berger, took the lead at the start and then broke down, handing Fabi the lead, but his car failed before the end of the same lap - and thus he never led a lap...

When it comes to records, being Italian seems to be a really bad idea. Nicola Larini, for example, holds the record for the number of races he took part in before scoring a World Championship point (44), while Luca Badoer holds the record for the most race entries without ever scoring a point (58) and, of course, there is the monster record of the most races by a driver without winning a race, which stands at 208 to the delightful but accident-prone Andrea de Cesaris. The Italians failed to get the record for the most races started by a driver before a first F1 victory, which currently stands to Mark Webber with 130 starts.

It is interesting to note that Nico Rosberg hold the record for the most GPs contested before winning a World Championship (206), while his father Keke has the record for the fewest F1 victories achieved before winning the World Championship. This stands at an astonishing one GP victory. Mike Hawthorn won the title in 1958 with only one victory that season, but he had won several races in previous years. Keke was champ after just one win, but would go on to achieve others.

There has been one occasion when the Constructors' World Championship runner-up did not win a single race, which was in 2004 when BAR-Honda achieved this remarkably unremarkable feat, while I am rather fond of Narain Karthikeyan's achievement as the only man ever to finish a World Championship Grand Prix in 24th place. No-one has done that before or since, despite the fact that there were 34 starters at the 1953 German GP - also a record.

Numbers

Before the start of the 2017 season, there had been 956 World Championship Grands Prix (Grandes Épreuves, as they are known) since the very first took place at Silverstone on 13 May 1950, with King George VI and his wife Queen Elizabeth (later to be known as the Queen Mother) turning up to watch.

The number of Grands Prix per year has steadily increased and, it seems, will continue to increase, and it is interesting to note that there were more than twice as many races in the 2000s as there were in the 1950s.

The actual breakdown is as follows: 84 races in the 1950s, 100 in the 1960s, 144 in the 1970s, 156 in the 1980s, 162 in the 1990s and 174 in the 2000s. Before the start of the 2017 season, there had been 136 in the 2010s, so it is possible that the total by the end of the decade could be 200.

This means that the record for drivers taking part in GPs will probably go on rising. At the moment that record is held by Rubens Barrichello with 326 starts between 1993 and 2011. Of the active drivers in 2017, Fernando Alonso is the closest (now Jenson Button has retired) with 274 starts, which means he needs at least three more seasons to catch and pass Rubens. By the end of 2017, both Kimi Raikkonen and Felipe Massa should get to over 270 starts as well, but it is hard to imagine either still being in action to beat Rubens's record.

Off track, there are people in the F1 paddock who reckon they have attended 750 Grands Prix. This means they must have started in the mid-1960s – and not missed a single race. There are quite a number, the author included, who have attended 500 races or more. That's easier than it used to be because if one was at the first race in 1950 it would have taken until the end of 1990 (41 years) to reach 500 GPs. In comparison, someone who started at the first race in 1980 would have completed 500 Grands Prix midway through 2010, after "just" 30 years full time in the business.

If you started appearing at races at the beginning of 1990, you won't have got to 500 yet, but you'll get there in mid-2018, after 27 and a half years on the road.

Ferrari, incidentally, is reckoned to have started 929 Grands Prix of the 956, beginning at the second World Championship race at Monaco in 1950, eight days after Silverstone. This means the team has missed only 27 races in the history of the series, a pretty impressive record. McLaren has 801 starts and Williams 657, while Sauber is the only other active team in the big league, with 421 starts.

Ferrari has a decent win record as well, with a 24.1 percent start/win ratio, but that's not in the big league when compared to Brawn GP's 47.1 percent, while Mercedes is closing in with a 43.2 percent win rate. Do they compare? Ah well, statistics…

More numbers

Since the end of the 1974 season only one man has driven a Formula 1 car with the number 1, without being the World Champion. Who was it? And how did it happen? In the early years of the FIA Formula One World Championship, there was no such thing as a numbering system. The race organisers would give out numbers based on whatever they wanted to do. This was why, for example, the highest number ever seen in F1 was 136, which was given to East Germany's Rudolf Krause, who raced a Reif-BMW at the German GP in 1952. That race saw all the Grand Prix cars numbered above 100, a system which meant that each car in every race had a unique number. People may write in if I do not say that there was a Formula 1 car that carried the number 208 in 1974 when Lella Lombardi tried to qualify a Brabham BT42 in Radio Luxembourg colours (208 being the radio station's wavelength). She failed to make the field.

The number 13 was never used because of racing tradition, dating back to the 1920s, although cars with that number did appear in Mexico in 1963 with Moises Solana using it for his BRM P57 and in 1976 when Divina Galica used the number for her Surtees TS16, but failed to qualify for the race.

The lowest Formula 1 number used was 0, which has only been used twice since 1974 – when a World Champion moved from the team with which he won the title. This happened in 1993 and 1994 with Williams as Nigel Mansell and then Alain Prost both left Williams as World Champions. As a result, Williams had the right to use numbers 1-2 because it had won the Constructors title in the previous year, but the lead driver did not have the right to use number 1, because he was not the World Champion. Thus in 1993 Prost used number 2, while Damon Hill was given 0, and in 1994 Ayrton Senna (and his successors) used number 2, while Hill continued to use 0.

In 1973 Jody Scheckter used 0 in the final two races of the year, when he was driving a third McLaren.

The lack of numbering system lasted only until 1973 when it was decided that it might be an idea to keep the same numbers. This began to happen in the second half of the season and the numbers were then set in stone from 1974 onwards, with the only change each year being the number 1 and 2 being given to the World Champion and his team-mate in the season after he won the title. It began in 1974 with Ronnie Peterson running with #1 and Jacky Ickx with #2 for Team Lotus as a result of the team having won the Constructors' Championship in 1973. The 1973 World Champion Jackie Stewart had retired at the end of the season.

After that the previous World Champion would get the new World Champion's old number. Thus, for example, Alan Jones switched from 27 to 1 in 1981, while Gilles Villeneuve went from 2 to 27 because Ferrari took over the Williams numbers (27 and 28) and Villeneuve stepped up to be team leader after Jody Scheckter (previously #1) retired at the end of a very disappointing season. This system remained unchanged until the end of 1995 when the FIA decided it needed to clean up the system as there were fewer teams and the new operations had not taken over the numbers that had been left by older teams disappearing. Thus the numbering system became such that the World Champion and his team-mate took 1 and 2 the following season, while the other teams took their numbers according to their finishing position in the Constructors' Championship. This meant that teams could not easily use their numbers in marketing campaigns, because they would change year by year.

In the end, before the 2014 season the FIA agreed to allow the drivers to choose their own permanent numbers, with the #1 being left open for the World Champion, if he wanted to use it. The number 13 also appeared that year as Pastor Maldonado wanted to use it.

All of this means that since the start of 1975 only one driver has ever appeared in the #1 car who was not a World Champion. This was John Watson, who appeared at the European Grand Prix at Brands Hatch in 1985. He was standing in for Niki Lauda, who was out of action having suffered a wrist injury when he crashed in the Friday practice session at the Belgian Grand Prix. The steering wheel whipped around in the impact and Lauda's wrist was strained. It was felt best that he miss the next race and Watson was called up to help.

Strange, but true

Damon Hill and Sir Jackie Stewart share one of the oddest F1 records: they are the only two men in the 66-year-old history of the World Championship who have lapped all the other finishers TWICE.

And yet neither of these races account for the largest winning margin in the sport, which remains the 1958 Portuguese GP, which Stirling Moss won by 5m02.75s... despite Mike Hawthorn finishing on the same lap! This was caused by the fact that the Boavista street circuit in Porto was 4.6 miles long and Hawthorn drove a very slow last lap, without being under threat from anyone else.

Hill won the 1995 Australian Grand Prix in Adelaide by two complete laps. This, incidentally, is also deemed to have been the race with the highest official attendance figures, with 210,000 people present.

How did it happen? Well, reliability played a role. Damon's team-mate David Coulthard was leading early on, but he came into the pits too fast and crashed into the pit wall. Michael Schumacher (Benetton) and Jean Alesi (Ferrari) collided. Gerhard Berger's Ferrari expired. Heinz-Harald Frentzen's Sauber's gearbox lunched itself. Johnny Herbert's Benetton broke a driveshaft and Eddie Irvine's Jordan-Peugeot lost its hydraulics and so it was Olivier Panis's Ligier which was second, ahead of a delighted Gianni Morbidelli in his Footwork. And, of course, Damon drove very quickly.

Back in the summer of '69, Jackie Stewart had done the same at Montjuic in his Matra-Cosworth, on another day when reliability was important. That day the Lotuses of Jochen Rindt and Graham Hill both crashed heavily as a result of rear wing failures. Jo Siffert's Walker-Durlacher Lotus, Jack Brabham's Brabham and Chris Amon's Ferrari all had engine failures, while Jacky Ickx's Brabham suffered a suspension failure, leaving second place to Bruce McLaren's McLaren, with Jean-Pierre Beltoise third in the second Matra.

The Adelaide was 2.3 miles in length, about the same as Montjuic – both being half the length of Boavista.

The age of F1 drivers

Age is a troublesome subject with some racing drivers. The oldest Formula 1 driver in 2017 was Finland's Kimi Raikkonen at 37 years of age. Felipe Massa and Fernando Alonso were both 35 and Lewis Hamilton was 32. The only other current driver over 30 was Romain Grosjean. It is a sport for youngsters.

In recent times we have seen older drivers, Michael Schumacher retired at the end of 2012 at the age of 43. The same year Pedro de la Rosa retired at 41 and Rubens Barrichello was 39 when his F1 career ended in 2011.

In the old days of F1, the drivers were able to go on much longer than they do today. In fact, the oldest ever driver in a World Championship event was Monaco's Louis Chiron, who was 55 years old when he started the Monaco Grand Prix in 1955. Three years later he tried again, but that time failed to qualify at Monaco (as did one Bernie Ecclestone on the particular occasion).

Obviously 58 was just too old...

Chiron's achievement was not that much more than the previous record holder, France's Philippe Étancelin, who raced in the French GP in 1952, when he was 55. At that point he had already established the record for being the oldest driver to score a point, having finished fifth at Monza in 1950 in a Talbot, at the age of 53. The oldest race winner was Luigi Fagioli, who won the 1951 French GP at 53 years of age, and the oldest World Champion was Juan Manuel Fangio in 1957, at the age of 46.

In the modern era we have seen Damon Hill win the title at 36, Mario Andretti and Alain Prost at 38, and Nigel Mansell and Graham Hill at 39. The only man to win the title over 40 since the 1950s was Jack Brabham in 1966.

Jack celebrated his 40th birthday in April that year, before the World Championship began. He won the International Trophy at Silverstone but his first World Championship victory did not come until the French GP in July. He then won the British GP a few days later and was suddenly in the running for the title. Some newspapers made a fuss about his age and so at the Dutch Grand Prix in late July at Zandvoort Jack thought he would take the mickey out of the media by appearing on the grid, wearing a false beard and hobbling to his car with a walking stick, pretending to be old. He then proceeded to lead the race. When he began lapping backmarkers he was badly baulked and Jim Clark managed to catch and pass him, but then the Lotus-Climax began to have engine vibration problems which led to a water pump failure. That put Jack back in the lead and by the end of the race the old man had lapped the entire field...

A question of nationality

Three of the 33 FIA Formula 1 World Champions were not born in the country under whose flag they raced. If they had been, Germany's first World Champion would have been in 1970, rather than 1994; Italy would have had a third World Champion, to stand alongside Nino Farina and Alberto Ascari, and Sweden would not still be waiting for its first F1 title holder…

By the same token, Niki Lauda would have been Austria's only World Champion, Phil Hill would be the only American to have won the world title and Finland's list of World Champions would be rather shorter…

How so? Well, Michael Schumacher's claim to be the first German World Champion would not be valid because Karl Jochen Rindt, born in Mainz in April 1942, would have beaten him to it by 24 years.

Rindt's father Karl was a 40-year-old German spice merchant, his mother was 29-year-old Austrian called Ilse Martinowitz. The pair lived in Mainz but were killed in July 1943, during the fire bombing of Hamburg, while they were away from their new baby, visiting the city. Rindt and his half brother Uwe Eisleben were sent to Austria and brought up by their maternal grandparents in Graz. They took Austrian nationality as a result…

Italy's third World Champion could have been Mario Andretti, who was born to Alvise and Rina Andretti in the village of Montona in Istria in 1940. At the time this area was part of Italy, although after the war it became Yugoslavia. Today it is part of Croatia. At the end of the war the Italian settlers in Istria, who had arrived after it became part of Italy in 1919 (having previously been part of the Austro-Hungarian Empire), were ordered out by the Yugoslav government. After spending time in a refugee camp in Italy, the Andretti family went to the United States when Mario was 14. They settled in Nazareth, Pennsylvania, and he became a naturalised US citizen in 1964. Mario is motor racing's perfect example of the American Dream coming true…

Sweden's theoretical World Champion is none other than Keijo Erik Rosberg, who was born to Finnish parents in Solna, a suburb of Stockholm. Keke's father Lars Erik, known as Lasse, had moved there so as to study to be a veterinarian, because Finland did not get its first veterinary college until 1945, by which time Lasse was 23 and in the middle of his studies in Sweden. He went home for the holidays and in 1946 married Lea Lautaka, known as Lessu. She joined him in Stockholm and young Keijo appeared in 1948, although following the family tradition he took on a different name… They returned to Finland once Lasse had qualified.

Of course, if Keke had been Swedish then perhaps his son Nico would not have ended up being German.

Nationalities can be complicated sometimes…

Collecting the prizes

One can argue about the number of Finns who have won the FIA Formula 1 World Championship. In Abu Dhabi in 2016, Nico Rosberg, who raced with a German licence, but lived in Monaco most of his life, declared: "I have a Finnish passport as well. A part of me is Finnish and always will be and I'm very proud of that…"

A few days later, at the FIA Prizegiving Gala, held at the Hofburg Palace in

Vienna, Rosberg announced his retirement from F1 and then took to the stage the same evening to collect his trophy. In fact, he was the fifth Finn to collect the FIA Formula 1 Drivers' World Championship trophy.

Keke Rosberg, Mika Hakkinen and Kimi Raikkonen were all unquestionably Finnish World Champions. Nico Rosberg was German-Finnish, but he counts as well. So who was the fifth Finn to be given the F1 trophy?

No, it isn't a trick question. In 1970, Jochen Rindt won the World Championship. Sadly, he was killed at Monza in September but he had sufficient World Championship points to remain ahead, despite the fact that there were three races remaining. As a result, he became the first, and hopefully the only, posthumous Formula 1 World Champion in history. It was logical that his widow should be awarded the trophy in his honour. Nina Rindt was Finnish, the daughter of Curt Lincoln, the most celebrated racing driver in Finland in the 1950s, although he was a Swedish citizen until the 1960s.

Nina, incidentally, would later marry British aristocrat Alexander Hood and assumed the title, the Viscountess Bridport of Cricket St Thomas.

A most unusual prize

At every FIA Prizegiving Gala, the Formula One Constructors' Association Award is given to the best race promoter of the year. It is a little known fact that this was designed and made by one of Great Train Robbers. Known in the criminal world as "The Weasel", Roy James was a villain, best known as a getaway driver, but he had many other skills as well.

Born in Fulham in 1935, James grew up keen on sports. He excelled in waterskiing and was a top British contender in the late 1950s, while he also had a trial for the QPR football team. From quite early on, however, he used his athletic prowess as a cat burglar, who would scale buildings and break into apartments to steal jewellery and other valuable items. He was also a car thief and at one point nicked a Jaguar belonging to Mike Hawthorn. He used the car for a robbery and then left it parked near a celebrated racing club so that it would be returned to Hawthorn.

He had learned to be a silversmith, which was a useful talent for a cat burglar as he didn't need to pass on stolen goods and could simply melt down precious metals and create new products to sell, without fear of the object being recognized. Some of his work was sold by Harrods and he settled down to work, ostensibly, as an antique dealer, living in the chic Nell Gwynn House on

Sloane Avenue in Chelsea.

He began racing karts in 1960 and quickly became a top star in the relatively new sport. On one occasion he discharged himself from hospital after a car crash to race for Britain against the French at Carpiquet, near Caen. He was then 25 and had dreams of being a Formula 1 driver. He used crime to fund his racing, notably with a couple of profitable robberies on the Cote d'Azur. He then began an association with a group known as the South West Gang, led by Bruce Reynolds, a talented heist organizer. In 1962 the gang stole the BOAC airline payroll in dramatic fashion at Comet House in Heathrow Airport. It was a violent attack with several security men being clubbed unconscious by the gang and then the money being put into a Jaguar driven by Micky Ball, with a second car, driven by James, running interference if they were chased. At one point a car tried to block a gateway and James used his Jaguar to knock it out of the way. Similarly, he blocked a junction when faced with a red light, allowing Ball to motor through. The police would later arrest both men but James got away with it. Ball got five years.

James used his share of the money from that robbery to buy a Brabham BT6 Formula Junior, paying for the car with cash, and he raced in 1963 against the likes of Denny Hulme, Peter Arundell, Brian Hart, Frank Gardner and Alan Rees. He won one round of the national championship and a string of other events.

In August the South West gang, in league with another gang from the Brighton area, hit the Aberdeen-London mail train, using a rigged signal at Ledburn, south of Leighton Buzzard. James uncoupled the back carriages of the train, where mail sorters were working, and the front section of the train left them behind and stopped a few miles further down the line at a bridge over a country road near Cheddington. The gang smashed their way into the High Value Mail coach and, with military precision, transferred 20 mail bags to a truck and two Land Rovers. These were then driven to Leatherslade Farm, near Brill, not far from Bicester. The robbery netted an astonishing £2.6 million, about £38 million at modern prices.

The plan was to stay at the farm for two weeks, but the police guessed that the gang must have a hideaway and began searching the region. The gang dispersed rapidly, each robber taking £85,000, which is about £1.2 million at today's value. James gave £12,500 of his share to Ball's wife, and then returned to his normal activities in Chelsea.

The police went over the farm carefully and found James's fingerprints on a Pyrex plate, a St Johns Ambulance first aid kit and on a page of an American movie magazine. He turned up at Goodwood, for the next race and completed practice but then failed to appear for the race itself because the police had issued wanted posters for the gang.

For two months he disappeared but in December a woman informant told the police that James was hiding out in St John's Wood and even gave them details of a planned escape route he had. The police raided the flat and James was arrested, after a rooftop chase. In April 1964 he was sentenced to 30 years in prison at Aylesbury Crown Court.

He served 11 years, being released in 1975. He was then 40 and the money from the robbery was gone, used it seems by his criminal friends. He went to see the new boss of Brabham, Bernie Ecclestone, who told him it was too late for a serious racing career, but gave him the job of creating a new trophy. Others helped him to get a Formula Ford car and he did well and was looking to move up to Formula Atlantic in 1976. That summer he was testing a Lola at Silverstone when he put a wheel on the grass and crashed, breaking a leg.

That was the end of his racing dreams. He went back to making trophies and probably some less-than-legal activities. In 1984, at the age of 48, he married an 10-year-old, Anthea Wadlow, ironically the daughter of a bank manager, but soon afterwards he was arrested for allegedly importing gold, without paying duty. He was acquitted on that occasion, but in the years that followed his marriage broke down. He won custody of their two children but he failed to pay a £150,000 settlement to Anthea. This resulted in a confrontation between James and her father David Wadlow, and ended up with James shooting him several times and injuring his ex-wife as well. He turned himself in and was sent to jail for six years in 1994 for attempted murder.

He soon began to have heart problems which led to a triple bypass operation and early release from prison in 1997, but he died of a heart attack later that year, at the age of 62.

One wonders where he got the silver for the trophy…

A most unusual person

Jean-Marie Balestre, the FIA President, was a strange man. He was passionate about motor racing, he was very patriotic, he fought hard for what he believed in and yet, at the same time, his life history suggested that he was not a man who could be believed or trusted. There were too many contradictions - and too many people who swore blind he was a charlatan. Balestre sued whenever he was challenged and he won, but judges often gave him derisory sums in damages, a way for them to tell the world that they didn't believe a word of it. But, legally, his defence could not be beaten.

Balestre's strange stories, which were included in his cv, began with a claim that he fought with the communist-organised International Brigades in the Spanish Civil War, which began in June 1936. At that time Balestre, born in 1921, had only recently turned 15. The International Brigades were disbanded in September 1938, when Balestre would have been 17.

At the same time he claimed to have studied law before becoming a sports journalist in 1938, which makes no sense at all, as he was barely out on school and too young to study law at university. His cv says he was then in the French military during the Battle of France, but French police records show he was arrested for "escroquerie" (fraud) in 1940 and was only liberated when the Germans arrived in Paris in June. Two months later he helped Robert Hersant establish the Jeune Front, a pro-Nazi organisation, funded by the Germans. After that the two men set up a pro-Vichy training camp named after Marshal Petain in the Paris suburbs. Then in May 1943, at the age of 22, Balestre joined the Waffen SS. Of this there was no doubt. There are official SS documents, photographs and even articles in the French SS magazine, signed by SS Sergeant Balestre.

After the war Balestre claimed that he had joined the SS, working undercover for the resistance, but explained that all those who could verify his story had been killed. No one could prove this was not the case - with defamation it is not a question of reasonable doubt.

Balestre claimed he was arrested by the Germans in May 1944 and was sent to Dachau. Others insist he was arrested by the Americans a few months later and was in Dachau after it had become an Allied detention centre. Resistance people insisted he was SS and not a resistant. When he returned to Paris in May 1945, he was arrested and would spend two years on remand before being sentenced to a 10-year loss of civil rights for collaboration. Hersant suffered a similar fate, but was rehabilitated by an amnesty in 1952. He admitted what he had done and said it was down to youthful errors. Balestre denied everything and sued anyone who suggested otherwise. During the 1950s he collected official certifications that he had been a resistant. His critics said these had been purchased.

Balestre and Hersant went into business together in the publishing world in the late 1940s, and built up a publishing company that would ultimately include the newspaper *Le Figaro*. Together they formed *AutoJournal* and Balestre followed his passion for motorsport and played a huge role in establishing karting in France. He was the first President of the International Karting Commission of the FIA (CIK) and a founder member of the Federation Francaise du Sport Automobile (FFSA) and became its President in 1973. He quickly became a major player with the FIA, getting control of the sporting commission and turning it into the Federation Internationale de Sport Automobile (FISA). This then battled for control of the commercial rights of F1 with FOCA, led by Bernie Ecclestone and Max Mosley. The result was a compromise which gave Ecclestone commercial control of F1, but the FIA retained ownership of the rights.

In 1986 Balestre became president of the FIA and did much to fight for safety, despite opposition from teams and the industry. He was bombastic and hated those who stood up him. He once labelled Jean Todt, "the Napoleon of the sands" after a dispute over the Dakar Rally. Todt called him "the Emperor Bokassa of the Place de la Concorde". But his involvement in post-race politics after the famous collision between Ayrton Senna and Alain Prost in 1989 undermined his credibility and he was beaten in an election for the role of FISA President by Mosley although the two then worked together to merge the FIA and FISA and Mosley became FIA President. Balestre stayed on as president of the FFSA until 1996 and then quietly retired.

He never did manage to convince people he had not been a Nazi and, now and then, at the end of a long evening, he might quietly admit that he had done things in his youth that he regretted in later life. He died in 2008, at the age of 87. By then the world had moved on and no-one bothered to write a biography - without any fear of being sued.

Another story about prisons

Schloss Colditz is an imposing edifice, near Chemnitz in Saxony. It is famous because in World War II it was used as a maximum security prisoner of war camp - to house POWs who had repeatedly made escape attempts from other Nazi camps.

 This was a triumph of flawed thinking because by concentrating the talents of the best escapers in one place, the Germans created expertise that led to a constant stream of daring and clever escape attempts. The prisoners of Colditz would later become famous because of a series of books and a TV series about their exploits.

The ultimate achievement of these extraordinary men was the construction of a glider, hidden away in the attics above the castle's chapel, it was built behind a false wall and was designed to be launched from the roof top and to carry two men away from the castle, across the river below and into the valley beyond, from where they could set off for Switzerland. The glider was nearly completed when the American Army liberated the camp on 16 April 1945.

The idea of the glider came not from an airman, as one might expect, but rather from a 26-year infantry subaltern, who had served with the Rifle Brigade in the vicious battle for Calais in 1940.

The son of a Brigadier, Anthony Rolt was educated at Eton and at the Royal Military Academy at Sandhurst. He started competing in cars at 16 in speed trials and at 20 won an impressive victory in the British Empire Trophy at Donington Park in 1939, driving an ERA.

His nascent career as a racer was cut short by the war, but he was soon in the thick of the action, with the British Expeditionary Force in France. When the German attack began, he found himself as part of the small force defending Calais against the 10th Panzer Division. Their job was to delay the advance on Dunkirk, giving the Allies more time to evacuate large numbers of troops. Those who survived the Battle of Calais were taken prisoner.

Rolt dedicated himself to escaping and causing as much trouble as he could. After seven escapes - one of which got him to within sight of the Swiss border - he was finally sent to Colditz. When he returned to Britain after the war he discovered that he had been decorated with a Military Cross in Calais and a second for his escape activities. He had also been promoted to Major.

He was 26 and immediately began working with engineer Freddy Dixon on four-wheel drive systems, forming Dixon Rolt Developments, which pioneered the viscous coupling. This soon attracted backing from the tractor magnate Harry Ferguson and the business became FF Developments. Rolt continued to race and took part in the very first F1 World Championship race at Silverstone in 1950. This led to an opportunity to drive a factory Jaguar sports car and in 1953 Rolt and his team-mate Duncan Hamilton shared victory in the Le Mans 24 Hours in a C-Type.

Later FF Developments built a 4WD F1 car to demonstrate the possibilities of four-wheel drive technology. Rolt drove the car himself, but the Ferguson P99 car would go on to win the non championship Gold Cup at Oulton Park in the hands of Stirling Moss. It is the only 4WD car ever to win an F1 race. FF Developments sold its technology into the motor industry in the years that followed and Tony Rolt became a very wealthy man.

He died in 2008, at the age of 89, one of the last surviving drivers of the first World Championship Grand Prix. It was a life well-lived.

On the other side

The Victoria Cross is the highest award for bravery in the British military, and was formerly the highest available medal for troops from the British colonies. It is awarded for "most conspicuous bravery, or some daring or pre-eminent act of valour or self-sacrifice, or extreme devotion to duty in the presence of the enemy". There have been only 15 such awards in the last 70 years. In total, 182 VCs were awarded in the course of World War II.

Two VCs were awarded to New Zealanders during the Battle of Crete in May 1941. One to Second Lieutenant Charles Upham, who would win a second VC in Egypt 14 months later; the other to Sergeant Clive Hulme.

Hulme was a farm labourer, who before the war had worked on his parents' tobacco farm at Motueka, near Nelson, on South Island. He was something of a mystic, being a water diviner and a fortune-teller. When war broke out he and his brother Harold joined the 2nd New Zealand Division and were sent to Crete. They were there when the Germans launched a parachute assault on the island. Harold was killed while Clive began a startling career as a sniper, often behind enemy lines. His personal battle with the Germans lasted eight days during which killed at least 33 German snipers, and ended with him being shot in the shoulder during the Allied evacuation. He returned home a national hero, settling on North Island with his family, including his five year old son Denny Hulme, who would later become the 1967 Formula One World Champion.

Hulme told his son that he never worried about being shot because he knew he would survive the battle – and believed that the bullets bent around him..

They fly on the ground, they fly in the air

There has long been a link between fighter pilots and racing drivers, right back to the days when the very first flying machines left the earth. Among the pioneers of aviation were daredevil drivers like Maurice and Henri Farman, Albert Guyot, Arthur Duray and René Thomas (who survived his plane having a structural failure during an air show and plummeting 600 ft to the ground).

The First World War created a whole new generation of pilots who became racing drivers. France's biggest pre-war star, Geoges Boillot, was shot down and killed during the Battle of Verdun, but the country's biggest post-war star, Robert Benoist, was a fighter pilot, as was his rival Albert Divo. America's Eddie Rickenbacker was the highest-scoring ace of World War I and raced extensively, while Italy's "Meo" Costantini was also an ace, as was Caberto Conelli. Britain's Henry Segrave flew with the Royal Flying Corps and Germany's Ernst Burggaller flew with the Red Baron.

The link between the two roles continued until the age of the jet, after World War II. Aviation required the same kind of skills and courage as racing cars, or to put it another way, they were all slightly crazy.

I will eventually tell the tale of Tony Gaze, but for now I want to concentrate on Johannes Leonardus Flinterman, known as Jan, who shares the honour of having been the first Dutch F1 driver with Dries van der Lof, the pair having raced in the first World Championship Dutch Grand Prix in 1952.

Flinterman was a rather larger-than-life character and his record of two "kills" as a fighter pilot seems nothing exceptional until one understands that his speciality as a pilot was high-speed, low-level ground attacks. It was his ability to "go low" which earned him the the nickname "Crazy Flin" from his fellow pilots - suggesting that he was rather more daring than the average.

Flinterman was born in the Hague at the end of 1919 and wanted to join the Royal Dutch Navy to become a pilot when he was 16. At the time he was rejected because his eyesight was not reckoned to be good enough and so he served in a motorised unit of the Dutch army until the German invasion of the Netherlands in 1940. He was one of tens of thousands of Dutch military who were evacuated to England, getting across the Channel from the Hook, aboard HMS Keith, which was sunk a few days later off Dunkirk.

The need for pilots was such that Flinterman was taken on by the RAF, despite his nationality and despite his eyesight. He trained to fly in the course of 1941 and once he had his wings he was posted to Malta to join 126 Squadron, initially with Hurricanes and later with Spitfires. He would be on the island throughout the celebrated siege of Malta, spending most of his time attacking naval targets, trying to help ships get through to the island. It was not until the siege was over in June 1943 that he was sent back to Britain, to become a member of the newly-formed 322 (Dutch) Squadron, flying Spitfires. This was based initially at RAF Woodvale, near Liverpool, providing defensive cover over the Irish Sea, but it later moved south for convoy patrol work and then underwent training to work with the army on ground attacks.

In May 1944 Flinterman moved to 222 (Natal) Squadron as a Flight Lieutenant. The squadron flew support missions for the D-Day landings and then moved to Normandy and followed the allied armies east until the end of 1944, when it returned to the UK to convert to Tempests, before returning to the continent for the final months of the war.

In the summer of 1944 Flinterman was awarded a Distinguished Flying Cross for an aerial battle over Paris in which he and his flight shot down six of 14 German planes, despite being seriously outnumbered. He would add the Dutch Vliegerkruis (Flying Cross) and the Order of Orange-Nassau to his decorations before the end of the war, when he switched to flying Meteor jets before leaving the RAF to become head of the Dutch fighter pilot school and later the commander of the Volkel air base.

In the post-war era he was finally able to indulge in motor racing, initially in

500cc races but then in more powerful machinery, with a Kieft and then a Cooper. In 1952 the FIA agreed to give the Netherlands a Grand Prix race, at the Zandvoort circuit and several invitations to compete were extended to Dutch drivers. Flinterman organised to drive a third Maserati for Chico Landi's Brazilian team - Escuderia Bandierantes, alongside Brazilians Landi and Gino Bianco. The other Dutchman in the field was Van der Lof, in a third HWM. Flinterman's car retired early with a broken differential, but he then took over Landi's car and finished ninth.

It would be his only Grand Prix, but he continued to race for a while before leaving the air force in the late 1950s, to become an executive and board member of Martin's Air Charter, a freight airline which was later acquired by KLM and became Martinair Holland.

The stuff of (untrue) legend

Sydney Green was a one-armed fighter pilot who set up a racing team and built a Formula 1 car. What a ripping yarn!

Surf around the Internet and you can find it told here and there. You can read wonderful tales about how Greene was a decorated Spitfire pilot, who had several "kills" and was nicknamed "the Wingless Wonder" …until you look it all up in the official records and find that none of it stacks up – at least not in the way the story has been told.

Sydney George Greene was appointed a supernumary Flying Officer in the Royal Air Force Volunteer Reserve (Training Branch) in 1947, and was later given the rank of Squadron Leader, but that was after the war. During the conflict itself, he served with the Royal Observer Corps, a civil defence organization, administered by RAF Fighter Command. The ROCs wore RAF uniforms. Greene was an aircraft recognition instructor and obviously a valuable one.

The sobriquet "Wingless Wonder" was not applied because he had lost an arm, as the stories suggest, but rather was the term applied within the RAF to all officers who were not pilots – because they did not have wings stitched on their uniforms, as the pilots did. Call it journalistic license, but sometimes the facts are not as good as the resulting story. Nonetheless, Greene did good service for his country – as much as could be expected from a man with only one arm.

Born in Plaistow, in East London in 1908, Sid was 16 years old when he was knocked off his bike by a bus and lost his left arm. It was a devastating blow for the young apprentice, but he responded with remarkable determination and became a draughtsman, a job which allowed him to buy an MG Magnette with which he started motor racing. He did not adapt the controls, he simply drove the car with only his right hand!

When the war came, he was rejected by the British Army, which is not really surprising.

After the war, in addition to his RAFVR activities, he went into partnership with Monty Gilby to set up a business called Gilby Engineering. This grew rapidly in the 1950s, doing sub-contract work for big companies, such as Armstrong, Ford and CAV. Gilby returned to racing but soon switched to become an entrant. His biggest triumph was when Stirling Moss won the 1961 British Empire Trophy at the wheel of a Gilby Frazer Nash. The team also ran cars for the likes of Mike Hawthorn, Ivor Bueb and Roy Salvadori. The last-named raced a Gilby Engineering Maserati A6GCS sports car in 1953 and the following year Gilby took delivery of the first privately-owned Maserati 250F, which won a few minor races in Britain. This was followed by a Cooper-Maserati. Salvadori would later be replaced by Sid's son Keith who first got a racing licence in 1955. Sid wanted Keith to be a racing star.

In 1960 Sid hired ex-Lotus designer Len Terry who designed a 1098cc Gilby sports car for Keith to drive. This was prepared by Peter Ashcroft (later to become Competitions Manager for Ford GB) and Terry Hoyle, who became a celebrated engine builder in rallying. The Gilby-Climax produced a series of good results in the hands of the young Greene and Peter Arundell and so Sid decided to build a Formula 1 car for his son to drive in the new 1.5-litre formula.

Terry produced an uncomplicated design, powered by a Coventry Climax engine. The car showed particularly well when Gilby talked Bruce McLaren into giving it a test run.

The problem was that Gilby Engineering did not have a budget to do all the big races and so it appeared only in British events and one or two others. It finished fourth in the Lewis-Evans Trophy at Brands Hatch and sixth in the Danish Grand Prix at the Roskildering. There were good results in 1962 as well but a switch to BRM engines did little to improve the car. At the same time, Gilby Engineering had been acquired by another company, which was not interested in racing, and so the team was disbanded and the F1 car sold to Ian Raby.

Keith went on to find his niche not as a driver, but as a celebrated team manager for a wide variety of organisations in differing racing categories. Sons cannot always be what their fathers want them to be.

A proper flyer

While racing drivers are often fairly wild individuals, with a very different appreciation of danger compared to normal people, there were many others in F1 who were buccaneers by nature, be they team bosses, engineers, officials or media. BBC Formula 1 commentator Raymond Baxter may have appeared to be a fairly conventional individual - but he had adventurous genes.

Expelled from school for smoking, Baxter had a decidedly unglamorous job with the London Water Board when war broke out in 1940. The conflict would transform his life. He joined the Royal Air Force and was sent off to learn to fly at a civilian flying school in Tulsa, Oklahoma, starting out with an open-cockpit Fairchild PT-19 trainer before moving on to the North American Harvard. He was sent back to Britain, did 17 hours with a Miles Master and then found himself in charge of a Hurricane. A few days later he was posted to 65 Squadron to fly Spitfires...

He was sent to Scotland, although by then the Battle of Britain was over. He would eventually be posted to join 93 Squadron in Sicily and took part in the Italian campaigns, being mentioned in despatches once, before returning to Britain for a spell as an instructor. Flying Officer Baxter returned to active service in September 1944 with 602 Squadron, which had an unusual role, using the Spitfire as a fighter-bomber, trying to stop V-2 rockets, by attacking the launch sites.

In March 1945 Baxter was one of six pilots who took part in a daring daylight raid on the Shell-Mex building in The Hague, the command centre for V2 rockets. This was conducted flying at 400mph, at 100 ft. The bombs were released 50 yards from the target - when the planes were flying below rooftop level! Two of the six were hit by flak, while Baxter took a metal cockerel off the top of a church spire, next to the target. The raid earned him a second mention in despatches...

When the war ended, he joined the British Forces Broadcasting organisation in Cairo and later in Germany, becoming the deputy director of what had by then become the British Forces Network. In 1950 he was offered a job with the BBC and quickly gained a reputation as a frontman who could not be ruffled. He became the BBC's motoring correspondent, a job he held for 16 years and he commentated on F1 for the BBC for many years, although the coverage was not consistent, usually consisting of only a few races each year. He also did circuit commentary and became an accomplished rally driver, competing on the Monte Carlo Rally no fewer than 12 times, six of them as a member of the BMC factory team. He also took part in a number of other international rallies.

He became director of publicity at BMC for a short time in the mid-1960s, while still presenting for the BBC, but the company was then taken over by Leyland and the role disappeared. He returned to full time work with the BBC.

In the course of his career he covered all manners of events, including the opening ceremony of the Olympic Games in 1960, the funeral of King George VI, the coronation of Queen Elizabeth and later the funeral of Winston Churchill.

His first science show called *Eye on Research* ran from 1959 to 1963 and then he become the first host of a new programme called *Tomorrow's World* from 1965 until 1977. His audience was often up to 10 million viewers each week. He also presented the BBC's coverage of Farnborough Airshows from 1950 until 1986 and reported on the first flight of Concorde.

After *Tomorrow's World* he faded from the limelight, his style being rather out of place in the 1980s, but he lived to the ripe old age of 84 - a good score for an adventurer...

A slightly different fighter pilot

The world of Grand Prix racing has always attracted extreme people. Team bosses have often been ambitious, aggressive and anything but normal. Sometimes they are plain dysfunctional. It is part of the attraction of the sport. It's a soap opera. And some of those who don't quite make it are just as extraordinary as those who do. Take Robert Cowell, for example. He was a strange one, as you will see.

He was born 1918 in Croydon, the son of the then Lieutenant Colonel Ernest Cowell, a prominent and decorated officer in the Royal Army Medical Corps on the Western Front during World War I. He would later be knighted but at that point he was a surgeon at Croydon General Hospital.

As Robert (Bob) was growing up, Croydon Aerodrome was developing into the first London Airport and the youngster was fascinated by the flying machines – and by automobile racing. He attended Whitgift School, played rugby and was a member of the school's Motor Club. Cowell left school at 16, in 1934, and joined the General Aircraft Company in Hanworth to learn about aviation technology.

A year later he joined the Royal Air Force as a cadet and learned to fly Tiger Moths at RAF Grantham. He was the youngest officer in the entire Royal Air Force, but he suffered from air sickness and was instantly invalided out. His dreams were smashed.

He set himself a new goal. He would run his own Grand Prix team and be a racing driver. He enrolled at University College, London, to study engineering, and began his racing with a class win on the Land's End Speed Trial, driving a Riley. He was often at Brooklands, helping out, gaining experience and by 1939 he three racing cars and drive one in the Antwerp Grand Prix that year. He also took up flying again and qualified for a civil licence…

And then the war came and he joined the Royal Army Service Corps, served in Iceland with the goal of getting back into the RAF. He achieved that after a little over a year. By then he had also married and soon had two daughters.

He flew Spitfires and had a series of adventures while flying reconnaissance missions. Shortly before D-Day he was fortunate to survive a failure of his oxygen supply which left him unconscious in the cockpit, flying over enemy territory. Incredibly, the aircraft stayed in the air, was not hit by flak nor attacked by fighters, and gradually descended until he regained consciousness while over the English Channel and he was managed to fly it back to RAF Gatwick.

A few months later, flying a Typhoon on a reconnaissance mission over Germany, his luck ran out. A direct hit from flak meant he had to make a forced landing and was captured and sent to Stalag Luft I, near Lubeck. He was a POW for five difficult months, he was starved but spent most of his time, planning the car he would when his Grand Prix team was up and running. He was liberated in 1945 and returned home. He was then 27.

He hooked up with whisky heir Gordon Watson and set up a coachbuilding firm called Leacroft in Egham and they created their own Cowell-Watson sports car, based on a Lea Francis chassis. They also ran an Alta Grand Prix car and both raced it in a variety of events.

At the same time he ran a construction company to generate money and even started a dressmaking firm. There was never enough money and Cowell was often in trouble with creditors. The Grand Prix car was never built and in 1951 the name Robert Cowell disappeared from the racing scene. Instead a Roberta Cowell started appearing.

It would later emerge that in May 1951 Bob Cowell underwent the first ever sex-change operation, performed by Sir Harold Gillies, the New Zealander known as the father of plastic surgery.

Cowell's businesses failed and Watson disappeared from the scene, but Roberta continued to appear from time to time, winning the Ladies prize at Shelsley Walsh in 1957.

The news of the operation broke in the press in 1954 and Cowell was paid considerable sums by newspapers and publishing companies as a result. But the money did not last long and grand plans for flying records failed and by 1958 Cowell was declared bankrupt. She increasingly became reclusive, living with another woman for many years. Her last appearance in racing was in 1972.

Largely forgotten by then, she spent her last year's living alone in Hampton, Middlesex, where she died in 2011, aged 93.

Horse power

In 1903 a Frenchman called René Hanriot, a merchant from Châlons-sur-Marne, aged 35, drove a Clément automobile in the infamous Paris-Madrid road race, which was stopped in Bordeaux after a series of fatal accidents. Hanriot made little impression that day, but in the years that followed he won various big races and finished second in the prestigious Circuit des Ardennes. For a few years he was a regular on the Grand Prix scene, but then aviation came along and he discovered a new passion. He set up his own company to manufacture aeroplanes, based at the Aérodrome de la Champagne at Bétheny, alongside the main road north out of the city of Reims. He also opened a flying school and in 1912 one of the pupils to pass through the school was a 24-year-old Italian by the name of Francesco Baracca. He was a cavalry officer in the 2nd Reggimento Piemonte Cavalleria, one of the most famous units in the Italian army.

Once he had his licence, Baracca went back to Italy and was transferred to the new Battaglione Aviatori. Italy did not enter World War I until April 1915 and at that point Baracca was sent back to Paris, to be trained to fly the new French-built Nieuport 10, a two-seater reconnaissance aircraft. This was not much use as a fighter aircraft and it was not until the Italians received the Nieuport 11 a year later that they could begin to engage with enemy aircraft on the Italian Front.

Baracca was the first Italian to shoot down an enemy plane – a Hansa-Brandenburg flown by an Austrian pilot. More and more victories followed and after his fifth triumph he officially became an ace. The tradition at the time was for the aces to decorate their planes with a crest or an emblem and Baracca chose a black prancing horse on a white background. There are various stories as to why he chose it: the first is that it was the regimental badge of the 2nd Reggimento Piemonte Cavalleria, which makes sense; but there is a second argument that he picked the symbol because he had shot down a German plane, which carried the coat of arms of the city of Stuttgart, a black prancing horse on a yellow background. Perhaps it was both. In May 1917 Baracca took command of the 91st Squadron, which was equipped with new SPAD VIIs. All the planes carried his prancing horse and in the months that followed he became a national hero. By September his total of confirmed victories had risen to 19 and by the start of 1918 it was at 30. It seemed that Baracca was invincible, but then in June 1918 he failed to return from a mission. His body was recovered a few days later when an Italian advance revealed his downed plane. When the war ended, a few months later, he was still Italy's highest-scoring ace of the war with 34 victories.

Five years later, in June 1923, Count Enrico Baracca, Francesco's father, was guest of honour for a motor race on the Savio circuit, near Ravenna. This was a fast triangle of public roads south of the city and it was won by a 25-year-old called Enzo Ferrari, driving a factory Alfa Romeo. Baracca presented Ferrari with the trophy and later Enzo visited the family and met Baracca's mother, Contessa Paolina. She suggested that he use the prancing horse logo on his racing cars. Ferrari was an Alfa Romeo driver at the time and the company had its famous Quadrifoglio – the four-leaf clover badge – on its cars. Scuderia Ferrari was not established until the end of 1930, seven years later, but it was still the Alfa Romeo factory team and it was not until July 1932 that Ferrari put his own version of Baracca's badge, with a yellow background, on his cars for the Spa 24 Hours. The two Alfa Romeo 8C 2300 MMs were driven to a 1-2 victory by Antonio Brivio/Eugenio Siena and Piero Taruffi/Guido d'Ippolito.

Oddly, the Prancing Horse also features in the Porsche logo, along with the word Stuttgart. It is a little known fact that the Ducati motorcycle company also used the Prancing Horse in the late 1950s and early 1960s because the company's chief designer Fabio Taglioni came from the village of Lugo, where Baracca was born.

Horses for courses

Engines can be used for many different tasks. The displacement can be changed, cylinders added or removed, and it is not unusual for two engines to be put together to create something quite different.

A recent Aston Martin V12, for example, can trace its roots back to Porsche in the 1990s, when the Stuttgart firm created a 60-degree V6 engine, but then decided not to use it for production cars. The design was sold to the Ford Motor Company and the resulting engine was called the Ford Duratec V6, an aluminum unit with dual overhead camshafts. The designers at Cosworth, which was then owned by Ford, mated two of these engines end-to-end and created the 6-litre V12, which ended up belonging to Cosworth and being used by Aston Martin in its 1999 DB7 Vantage.

It's a complex industry...

Enzo Ferrari's son Alfredo, known as Dino, had a tragically short career as an automobile engineer. Trained in various schools in finance, economics and engineering, Dino was supposed to succeed his father. He never finished his engineering studies, stopping after two years, because of illness. The family legend suggests that it was Dino who first suggested that Ferrari build a small-capacity V6 racing engine, at the end of 1955. Others say that the idea came from Vittorio Jano, who had already created the first production V6 engine, working on the Lancia Aurelia with Ettore Zaccone Mina, but that Dino Ferrari thought it was a good idea.

Dino died in June 1956, at the age of 24, and never saw the finished engine. It was a 65-degree 1.5-litre dual overhead camshaft V6. This was to form the basis of the company's modern V6 engines right up until the mid 2000s.

This engine was first raced in Luigi Musso's Ferrari 156 in the non-championship F1 Gran Premio di Napoli at Posillipo at the end of April 1957. Musso finished third behind the Lancia-Ferraris of Peter Collins and Mike Hawthorn. The following year the engine appeared in 2.4-litre form in the 246 Formula 1 car, the first V6 in F1. This was strong enough to win the 1958 French GP at Reims, in the hands of Mike Hawthorn. The engine was also seen in 2-litre form in the Ferrari 206S sports car and in 3.2-litre form in the Ferrari 326 MI, which Phil Hill drove in the one-off Monza 500 Miles, against visiting American machinery. The engine would continue to appear in F2 and when F1 switched to 1.5-litre regulations in 1961, the Dino V6 would be the engine that gave Ferrari another Formula 1 World Championship, with Phil Hill and Wolfgang Von Trips fighting for the title. In 1961 the 2.4-litre version appeared in the 246 SP, the first mid-engined Ferrari and in the mid 1960s in the Dino 166P and its successors the 206 S and 206 SP sports cars. The engine was then re-engineered by Aurelio Lampredi and was used in a series of production cars, beginning with the 1968 Dino 206 GT and the Fiat Dino.

After Ferrari production ended, the 2.4-litre version of the engine was given to Lancia and powered the Lancia Stratos rally car, which enjoyed much success in the World Rally Championship in the 1970s, winning titles in 1974, 1975 and 1976 in the hands of Sandro Munari and Bjorn Waldegard, including three wins on the Monte Carlo Rally.

The most experienced Ferrari F1 driver

Can you name the Ferrari driver who has driven the most number of different F1 cars for the celebrated Italian firm? Michael Schumacher, you might say. He was at Maranello for a long time. Or maybe Rubens Barrichello? Or perhaps it was Gerhard Berger… The answer might come as a bit of a surprise because it is a name that the majority of F1 fans have probably never heard before: Andrea Bertolini. He has tested every type of Ferrari F1 car from 1974 to the present day – with the one exception being the 126 C2, the car which won the 1982 Constructors' title, but missed the Drivers' title because of the death of Gilles Villeneuve and the crash that maimed Didier Pironi. In total, Bertolini has tested more than 350 different Ferrari F1 cars.

He shakes them down after they come in for maintenance and sets them up for the customers who have bought them. Bertolini began his career as a Ferrari apprentice at 17 and has spent his entire career with Ferrari at Maranello. He has enjoyed on-track success with Ferrari works GT cars, although he began as a humble mechanic, working on a test bench and racing karts as much as he could in his spare time. This drew him to the attention of Dario Benuzzi, Ferrari's chief test driver and he learned the skills required for the role from Benuzzi.

Benuzzi is another man whose F1 involvement has not been fully recognised. He has never raced, but joined Ferrari as a mechanic in 1971 and was soon working in the prototype division and became a test driver under the watchful eye of Roberto Lippi. He has been developing road cars since then, but he was also the primary Ferrari F1 test driver from the late 1980s (after the departure of Johnny Dumfries) until 1993, when Nicola Larini took over the role. Benuzzi handed over his production car testing role to Raffaele de Simone in 2013.

What could have been...

Getting hold of an engine was a big problem for aspiring Formula 1 teams in the early 1980s, when the Cosworth DFV era was coming to an end. Williams did a deal with Honda, Brabham signed with BMW, while Ferrari, Renault and

Alfa Romeo did their own things, but McLaren had to convince TAG to fund a Porsche engine. Most teams didn't have the money to do such things. The DFVs were not really competitive and the new generation turbos were powerful but unreliable. Manufacturers were not keen on doing customer deals.

Ted Toleman might have waited to see what would happen, but he was a man in a hurry. He had been building up a team in Formula 2, beginning in 1978, using March chassis and Brian Hart engines. The team switched to Ralts in 1979 and then in 1980 Rory Byrne designed Toleman's own F2 car. Brian Henton and Derek Warwick finished 1-2 in the European Championship.

It was time to step up into F1 and no-one was surprised when Toleman announced in November 1980 that it was entering F1. History relates that the team used a turbocharged version of the Hart F2 engine and that the Toleman TG181 was overweight, underpowered and unreliable. It took Henton and Warwick until September to qualify a car for a race.

What many forget is that Toleman came close to doing an engine supply deal with Lancia.

Four years earlier Fiat had decided to try to integrate its motorsport operations and an edict was sent out that the different marques should use motorsport to promote their production cars. Lancia motorsport boss Cesare Fiorio was told to use a car from the Lancia Beta range. This was not easy. The Betas were big solid-looking luxury cars, which had been launched in 1972. It was the first model introduced by Lancia after it was taken over by Fiat in 1969 and the goal was to focus on quality. The cars featured a straight four 2-litre engine designed by former Ferrari designer Aurelio Lampredi.

To make the range a little sexier Lancia launched a Montecarlo version of the car in 1975, a Pininfarina-designed mid-engined sports car. These did not sell well, but when Fiorio sat down with engineers Gianni Tonti and Giampaolo Dallara to try to figure out what to do, they concluded that Lancia Beta Montecarlo might conceivably be successful in the Group 5 sports car championship.

This had started in 1976 and was basically a silhouette formula, with standard production car bodies (but dramatic mudguards) and original engine blocks in the same location and the same orientation as the road cars. Other than that the engineers could do what they wanted.

The trio concluded that if they downsized the 1.8-litre straight four cast iron block used in the U.S. version of the Beta Montecarlo, mated it with a version of the Fiat 131 Abarth 16-valve aluminium cylinder heads, which had been used to win the previous year's World Rally Championship (and would go on to win that year and again in 1980) and added a big KKK turbocharger, they ought to have a competitive car in the 2-litre class, allowing for the 1.4 equivalency calculation for the turbo (1.4 x 1.4 = 1.96).

The 34-year-old Tonti set to work with help from Nicola Materazzi and they created the 14.78T engine. The new car – which bore little ressemblance to the road car – was launched in December 1978 and the first tests with the new engine took place in April 1979. That year Riccardo Patrese and Walter Rohrl won the Group 5 World title, a feat that Lancia then repeated in 1979 and 1980.

What Toleman wanted to do in 1980 was to upgrade the 1.4-litre turbo to a 1.5 – and get Lancia into F1. It didn't happen, probably because Enzo Ferrari objected to the idea.

Fiorio would get to F1 in the 1990s, as head of the Ferrari sporting department (after Enzo had died). Tonti would move on and design Alfa Romeo F1 turbos and Toleman would struggle until it was taken over by Benetton and was later transformed into Renault F1. For a while it turned into Lotus and is now Renault again…

One can only wonder what might have happened if there had been a Toleman-Lancia.

The Italian job

British influence at Ferrari is not new, dating back to the 1950s, when Mike Hawthorn and Peter Collins made a big impression, the former winning the World Championship for the Italian team in 1958.

A string of other British drivers raced for Ferrari, notably Tony Brooks, Cliff Allison, John Surtees, Mike Parkes, Jonathan Williams and Derek Bell. Then there was then a very long gap before Johnny Dumfries was signed up as a test driver in 1985 and four years later Nigel Mansell joined the team. And then, of course, there was Eddie Irvine.

There have been plenty of British engineers as well, from Parkes in the early 1960s to Harvey Postlethwaite, John Barnard, Ross Brawn, Pat Fry and James Allison.

What is often forgotten is that the team's first full monocoque chassis (as opposed to a semi-monocoque) was also built by John Thompson, who ran a company called TC Prototypes, in Weedon, a small village on the A5, in Northamptonshire…

At the time, it was 1972, Ferrari had not won an F1 World Championship title since 1964. The Italian fans were impatient.

The change to "the 3-litre formula" in 1966 saw the team introduce the Ferrari 312, designed by Mauro Forghieri, which was used until 1969. This was followed by the 312B in 1970 with which Jacky Ickx won three Grands Prix. This in turn was followed by the 312B2 in 1971 and the same car was revised for 1972. Ickx won the German GP that season, but Ferrari dropped to fourth in the Constructors' Championship and pressure for change grew.

Forghieri intended to take the world by storm with a new car with a full-width nose and square bodywork, unveiled in August 1972. The 312 B3, as it was known, soon earned the nickname "spazzaneve", meaning snowplow. It was tested by Jacky Ickx and Arturo Merzario and neither was impressed and Enzo Ferrari blew his top and banished Forghieri to the Special Projects department. Soon afterwards, team manager Peter Schetty decided to go back to his family's business in Switzerland.

In Forghieri's place, Ferrari appointed Sandro Colombo, a graduate of the Politecnico di Milano, who had worked mainly in motorcycle design, with Gilera, Bianchi, Ossa and then Innocenti, which he had joined in 1960. He got to know Ferrari in 1963 when Innocenti tried to make a sporting coupé, which was to be powered by a Ferrari engine. Later, when Innocenti was taken over by British Leyland, Colombo left and went to work at the Centro Ricerche Fiat in Orbassano, near Turin. He was then seconded by Fiat to Ferrari, joining the company in April 1972. He was 48 and a man who understood the practicalities of engineering. His conclusion was that Ferrari was being regularly beaten by British engineers and so the best thing to do was to go to the British to broaden the Italian team's knowledge. The spazzaneve project was discarded and a new full monocoque car was designed, although (oddly) it retained the same 312 B3 nomenclature, presumably to avoid embarrassment.

Colombo did some research and heard about the 32-year-old metal-working wizard who had been working in motorsport for a decade, initially with Bruce McLaren, where he first gained the reputation of being a magician. McLaren designer Robin Herd then took him to Cosworth to work on the engine firm's F1 car in 1969 before they both moved on to March Engineering, where Thompson worked on the early March designs.

At the end of 1970, however, Thompson decided to set up his own business, TC Prototypes, and work for whoever was willing to pay him.

A fortnight after the 1972 season ended, Colombo went to England for the London Motor Show at Earls Court. He arranged a meeting with Thompson at Weedon, and arrived with a briefcase full of drawings, asking Thompson how much it would cost to build three bare monocoque chassis. Thompson was impressed by the quality of the draftsmanship and jumped at the chance. This kept TC Prototypes busy that winter.

The F1 season in 1973 started in Argentina at the end of January and Ferrari had no choice but to use the old 312 B2s. Ickx was fourth in Buenos Aires and Merzario was fourth in both Brazil and South Africa, which followed. There was then an eight-week gap before the European season began in Spain. The three Thompson chassis had been sent out to Italy by then, but only one car was ready for Ickx and he finished a miserable 12th. There was still only one car for Belgium and Ickx retired with an oil pump failure. Ferrari returned to running two cars in Monaco, but both had mechanical failures and Ferrari began to lose heart. There was only one car sent to Sweden, although Ickx finished sixth and in France he was fifth with Merzario seventh, but then it was back down to one car again for the British GP. Ferrari then missed both the Dutch and German GPs as upheaval followed in Maranello. Colombo went back to Fiat and Forghieri returned from his exile. The car was revised in Austria, but Ickx had lost interest, although Merzario finished seventh. Ickx rejoined the team in Monza before leaving completely, so Ferrari sent only one car to the final two races. The Italians like to blame the poor season on the decision to buy a British product, but Forghieri retained the monocoque, even if he changed most of the rest of the car. Luca Montezemolo was called in to become the new sporting director and Ferrari abandoned its sports car racing projects, in order to concentrate solely on F1. New drivers, Niki Lauda and Clay Regazzoni, were hired from BRM.

It was easy to blame the "Thompson B3s" and Forghieri had no desire to give the English any credit, but the 1973 car provided him was a good starting point for the 1974 B3s, which were much more competitive and set the team on an upward path again.

Colombo became the product manager for the Fiat 131 and then moved on to become head of development at Magneti Marelli.

Fair play

In the 17th arrondissement in Paris there is a garage called Le Fair-Play. We'll gloss over the fact it sells Volkswagens and concentrate for now on the concept. It is not a very French expression and, remarkably, was imported from English – because the French did have a word for sportsmanship.

Back in the 1960s there was an amusing musical comedy duo called Flanders and Swann. They sang clever songs including one called "The Song of Patriotic Prejudice", which was amusingly rude about the other nations of the world and chorused with "The English, the English, the English are best. I wouldn't give tuppence for all of the rest". It made people laugh, not because they took it seriously – but because they understood it was a satirical look at nationalism.

One of the verses was about sports.

"And all the world over each nation's the same," it went. "They've simply no notion of 'Playing the game'. They argue with umpires, they cheer when they've won, and they practice beforehand – which ruins the fun."

The point – now long forgotten – was that, for the English, sport was not about winning, but rather about the pleasure of competition, and if your opponent played well and won, one was generous and applauded the achievement. It was born from the respect between competitors.

There have been two outstanding examples of sportsmanship in the history of F1, although these were long before the sport was played to Schumacher Rules, where shoving a rival off the road is deemed to be the norm. The first was at Monza in 1956, in the final race of the season. Argentina's Juan Manuel Fangio (45) was the favourite to win his fourth world title. His challenger was his Ferrari team-mate 25-year-old Englishman Peter Collins, who was in a position to become his country's first Formula 1 World Champion.

Fangio had an eight point advantage which meant that Collins had to win the race and set the fastest lap – without Fangio scoring. So it was really down to reliability.

As luck would have it, Fangio retired with steering problems. In those days, teams were still allowed to switch their drivers between cars and so Ferrari asked its third driver Luigi Musso to hand his car over to Fangio. He refused to do so, on the grounds that he didn't wish to disappoint his home crowd. This meant that Collins was on track for the title as he closed in on race leader Stirling Moss.

But then, with 15 laps to go, Collins slowed and drove into the pits. He handed the car over to Fangio, thus giving up any chance he had of winning the world title. Fangio rejoined, but could not catch Moss.

Collins said that Fangio was too great a driver to be let down by machinery, and added that he was still young and would win a title soon enough. Alas, that did not happen. Two years later Peter Collins died in an accident at the Nürburgring.

Three weeks after Collins's death, the Formula 1 teams gathered again for the Portuguese GP on the streets of Porto. The battle for the World Championship that year was between Moss in a Vanwall and Mike Hawthorn in a Ferrari. It was wet on the day of the race and Moss and Hawthorn fought for the lead, until Hawthorn spun and ended up on a pavement, off the race track. The car stalled. When Moss came around on his next lap, he shouted to Hawthorn to try to bump-start the car, by letting it roll down the hill behind where the

Ferrari had stopped. This worked, Hawthorn rejoined and finished second to Moss. After the race, the stewards decided to exclude Hawthorn because he had driven the wrong way on the race track. Moss heard the news, went to see the stewards, argued that Hawthorn had not been on the track and should not be disqualified. They reversed the decision and Hawthorn was given back his second place. Two races later Hawthorn won the title from Moss by just one point… thanks to Stirling's sense of fair play.

When Enzo calls...

Franco Lini did not intend to become a team manager. It just happened.

There is no school for Formula 1 team principals. They just come along and are in the right time and the right place - with the right sort of skills (or not) to meet the challenges of the moment. Some inherit the job, some buy their way to it, others work for decades to get there, or convince industry magnates that they are one for the job. And some just get asked…

Born in the city of Mantua in 1925, Lini was inspired to go racing by the exploits of Tazio Nuvolari, who was not only Italy's biggest star of they day, but also the father of one of Franco's schoolmates.

Going motor racing is not just about inspiration, of course, it's also about money and in this respect Lini was fortunate as his family owned a successful machine tool business and so he was able to enjoy a life of motorcycle racing, fast cars and lots of exciting women. In order to help fund his motorcycle races he ran a small weekly motorcycle magazine and he did his first reports on automobile races by chance when a Milan newspaper asked him for a report on the San Remo Grand Prix on the Ospedaletti street circuit on the basis that he would be there racing his motorbike.

This went well and further reports followed until, two years later, Lini crashed badly, broke his neck and decided as he was recovering that perhaps he was better suited to writing than to racing. He thus became a full time journalist and was soon very popular and well known as one of the few F1 writers who travelled to all the races around the world. It was a time when Alfa Romeo and then Ferrari and Maserati were leading the way, before the rise of the British F1 teams, and Lini was the big name in motorsport journalism in Italy. He became so knowledgeable, in fact, that one day in 1966, after Enzo Ferrari fell out with Eugenio Dragoni, and the Ferrari team was split by political battles, Ferrari complained about things Lini had written and the conversation ended up with Ferrari telling Lini he could have the job if he thought he could do better.

The dominant force at the time was the Brabham-Repco team and Lini knew that his first priority was to get a top driver to replace the departed Surtees. He picked Chris Amon to partner Lorenzo Bandini.

The 1967 season did not begin well, however, when Bandini crashed at Monaco and suffered terrible burns from which he died a few days later. Lini called in Mike Parkes as a replacement and he and Ludovico Scarfiotti shared victory in the non-championship Syracuse GP. The next race was Zandvoort, where the new Ford Cosworth engine appeared for the first time and Jim Clark won ahead of the two Brabhams with Ferrari 4-5-6.

At the time Ferrari was dividing the company's efforts between F1 and sports cars and although Parkes and Scarfiotti finished second in the Le Mans 24 Hours, Parkes then crashed his F1 car badly at Spa and suffered leg injuries that would end his driving career. For the rest of the summer Ferrari ran only one car, although the team tried Jonathan Williams in a second car in Mexico at the end of the year.

Lini was behind the hiring of rising star Jacky Ickx to partner Amon in 1968 and the Belgian won the French GP that summer and Derek Bell was also given a chance towards the end of the year, but that summer Enzo Ferrari agreed terms to sell the production car business to Fiat for $11m and was not focussing on the racing. Lini battled with him to try to get him to concentrate on F1 but in the end he gave up and resigned. Ickx departed as well.

Franco went back to journalism and continued to be an enthusiastic member of the F1 media until his death from lung cancer in 1996, shortly before his 72nd birthday.

Here today, gone tomorrow

Formula 1 is sometimes a world where people are "here today, gone tomorrow". There are some who stay for years on end, but many do not. And some come, have an important role for a short time, and then depart. Peter Schetty, the Ferrari F1 team manager, was one of these.

The Schetty family founded a dyeing company in Basel in the 1850s and built it into one of the biggest in the country. The family diversified into plastic manufacturing as well, so money was never short when Peter, the heir to the family business, was growing up. Born in 1942 in Basel, he studied for a degree in economics at St-Gallen and then a doctorate in political science in Vienna. While he was growing up he was passionate about skiing and was a top class competitor until he broke his ankle badly and switched to his other passion – car racing.

During his teenage years he had often "borrowed" the family car when his parents were out for the evening and had driven on the country roads in the region. When he was 19, he competed with a Volvo on the Freiburg hillclimb. His father Rudolf was none too pleased as he wanted his son to concentrate on his studies but in late 1965 a friend called Karl Foitek, a young Zurich garage owner who had competed in the 1950s and 1960s before building up a string of dealerships, originally with Alfa Romeo, Jaguar and Lotus, and later with Ferrari, Lamborghini and Maserati, loaned him a Lotus Elan and Schetty impressed everyone by finishing second in class on the Marchairuz hillclimb. Peter then purchased a Shelby Mustang 350 GT, and raced with Squadra Foitek in the European Hill Climb Championship, finishing second in the GT category.

This led to him being hired by Carlo Abarth to compete in hillclimbs in a factory car. In addition to driving, he soon became the team manager as well and won a string of victories, including the Nürburgring 500km in 1968. For 1969 he was hired to race for Ferrari, driving the unique Ferrari 212 E Montagna, a one-off spyder built on a Dino 206S chassis and powered by a 2-litre flat-12 engine, which had been developed from the 1512 F1 engine of 1964. Schetty dominated the 1969 European Hillclimb Championship, winning every race in which he took part. His course record on the Cote de Cesana-Sestriere would remain unbroken for 13 years. This led to Ferrari making Schetty a member of the Ferrari sports car team in 1970, racing alongside Jacky Ickx and John Surtees in 512s. He then became the development driver for the new 312 sports car and was named as Ferrari team manager in sports car and in Formula 1. He held the job for years, 1971 nd 1972, during which time the F1 team won three victories: with Mario Andretti in South Africa in 1971, Jacky Ickx in Holland later that year and Ickx in Germany in 1972.

At the end of 1972 his father, who was nearing retirement, called him back to the family business and Schetty disappeared as quickly as he had arrived. The family dye business were sold in 1984 and Schetty moved into finance, although today he continues to run a large company manufacturing glassfibre reinforced polyester pipes.

And if the name Foitek sounds familiar, it is because Karl's son Gregor was an F1 driver, without much success, in 1989 and 1990 with Eurobrun, Rial, Brabham and Onyx. The best result of his seven starts (from 22 entries) was seventh place in Monaco in 1990, when Eric Bernard grabbed sixth (and his first F1 point) by driving Foitek into the wall in the final laps of the race.

Being well-connected

Giuseppe Farina worked in the vineyards near the village of Cortanze d'Asti, in the hills of Piedmont, to the east of Turin, where they grow Moscato Bianco grapes and produce a sparkling white wine. It was hard work and in the 1880s large numbers of Italian farm workers left; 50,000 a year moved to France, many others went to America. But Farina and his wife and their ever-growing family decided to try their luck in Turin. They opened a wine shop and things went well, although they started running out of names for their children. They already had Giovanni, born in 1884, but nine years later added a Giovanni Battista, their 10th of 11 children. Giovanni Battista looked so like his father that they called him Giuseppino – little Giuseppe. This soon became "Pinin".

The older Giovanni left school and went to work at Marcello Alessio's coachbuilding company, the early supplier of car bodies to Fiat. He married and soon, in the family tradition, they had two sons: Attilio and Giuseppe, the latter named after his grandfather. On the day Giuseppe was born, at the end of October 1906, Giovanni and another brother Carlo set up the Società Anonima Stabilimenti Industriali Giovanni Farina, to build car bodies for the new industry. When Pinin was 12, he joined the company and was soon designing prototypes. When the First World War started the state-owned Società Anonima Meccanica Lombarda copied the design of an Austrian biplane called the Aviatik and commissioned Farina to build the bodies. The company would return to automobiles in 1919 with small Temperino voiturettes, one of which was soon owned by Giovanni's 13-year-old son Giuseppe, by then known as Nino. He would soon join his Uncle Pinin as a riding mechanic in local racing events. At 17 he did his first hillclimb at Aosta, driving a Chiribiri.

Although the family had money, he wanted to buy his own machinery and so used what money he had to speculate on the Milan stock exchange. He lost everything, but his father came to his rescue and bought him a couple of Alfa Romeos, which they both used to go racing. Nino went to university and studied political science, gained a doctorate and then did his military service in the cavalry and with a tank regiment. By the time this was all done it was 1932, and he was 26. By then Uncle Pinin had left the family business and started his own Carrozzeria Pinin Farina.

Nino's racing career did not get off to a good start. He was fast, but his first season ended with a heavy crash, facial injuries and a broken shoulder. By 1936, however, he had made sufficient an impression to be taken on by Enzo Ferrari, as an Alfa Romeo factory driver. He soon showed that he was ruthless and uncompromising. At the Deauville Grand Prix that year he collided with Marcel Lehoux and the French driver was killed. Two years later in Tripoli, the same thing happened with Hungarian László Hartmann. His rivals called him dangerous, others reckoned he was just a nasty bastard.

There are some drivers who believe that they will never be killed in a racing car, that they are protected by lucky charms or Virgin Marys. Farina was one of them. The Second World War interrupted his career. He served as a tank commander and then joined the family business, although he had no real interest and left the running of it to his brother Attilio.

As soon as the war ended, he was racing again in a private Maserati. He was 39. But the Alfa Romeo factory team wanted experienced drivers and so he was signed again. In 1948 he married the fashion designer Elsa Giaretto. She wanted him to stop racing, but he refused to do so and when Jean-Pierre Wimille was killed at the start of 1949, Farina became the Alfa Romeo team leader. It was good timing. The World Championship kicked off the following year. Farina won the first race and added victories at Bremgarten and Monza and became the very first F1 World Champion.

He was overshadowed by Juan Manuel Fangio in 1951 and moved to Ferrari in 1952, but was outraced by Ferrari's new star Alberto Ascari. At the start of 1953 there was tragedy when he swerved to avoid a spectator at the Argentine GP and went into the crowd, killing at least nine people. It had little effect on him. Later that year he won the German GP, the Spa 24 Hours and the Nürburgring 1000.

He moved to Lancia in 1954 as team leader but crashed on the Mille Miglia and broke his right arm. He returned six weeks later only to suffer severe burns to his legs when a mechanical failure set the car on fire during practice for a sports car race at Monza. He spent three weeks in hospital.

The 1955 season would be his last in F1 but the following year he went to Indianapolis and failed to qualify and then broke his collarbone in a sport car crash at Monza. He went back to Indy with a Kurtis-Offenhauser in 1957 but his back-up driver Keith Andrews lost control of the car while practising and was killed and the car destroyed. That was the end of his racing career. He remained reckless and in 1960 as lucky to escape from a road accident when he ran into a truck near the city of Biella. His passenger was killed.

A year later the Uncle Pinin, by then a legend in the automobile industry, legally changed his family name from Farina to Pininfarina. He would die five years later in April 1966, at the age of 73. Two months after that Nino set off from Turin to drive to Reims for the French GP. As he made his way through the mountains, towards Chambery, he skidded on some ice at Aiguebelle, slid into a telegraph pole and was killed instantly. His luck had run out.

A strange end

Vittorio Jano is today considered to have been one of the greatest motor racing designers. And yet, on the morning on Saturday, March 13, 1965, he shot himself at his home in Turin. No one knew why. He was 73.

Rosina, his wife of 40 years, was in the next room; he had no financial problems; he left no suicide note, only speculation that perhaps he had discovered that he was suffering from a disease and having seen his brother die from a cancer did not want to go through the same. There was speculation too that he was depressed, dark thoughts having been brought on by memories of his only son Francesco, although he had died 20 years earlier.

The son of a celebrated Hungarian-born engineer, Vittorio was involved in the early years of the automobile, working briefly with the Ceirano brothers before joining Fiat in 1911. Three years later he was a member of the Fiat Grand Prix team at Lyon.

After a war spent developing aero-engines, he led the design team of the Fiat 501 road car before company boss Giovanni Agnelli decreed that Fiat was going racing again, which it did with great success with driver Pietro Bordino. Jano would then move on to Alfa Romeo when Enzo Ferrari offered to double his salary. He designed the Alfa Romeo P2, one of the greatest Grand Prix cars in history, which won many races in the hands of Antonio Ascari, Giuseppe Campari and Tazio Nuvolari.

This was followed by the P3 which was up against stronger opposition, from the all-conquering German teams in the 1930s.

In 1937 Jano moved on to Lancia as chief development engineer and during the war years worked to create the first production V6 engine, which appeared in the Lancia Aurelia in 1950. Soon after that the firm decided to enter F1 and Jano designed the revolutionary D50, which appeared in 1954 but the money ran out and Lancia sold the F1 cars to Enzo Ferrari.

Jano rejoined Ferrari as a consultant. The cars, badged as Ferraris, would win a string of races in 1956, driven by Juan Manuel Fangio and Peter Collins.

A ghost story

Ghost stories are not a big thing in Formula 1 history, but in the summer of 1988 you did have to wonder. At the time, McLaren-Honda was dominating with its amazing MP4-4. To give you an idea just how dominant it was, at Imola the two McLarens both qualified in the 1m27s, Senna being 0.7s ahead of Prost (imagine that gap today), but the third fastest driver was the World Champion Nelson Piquet in his Lotus-Honda. This matched the McLarens through the speed traps but was more than three seconds a lap off pole position. That is a huge car advantage and with Alain Prost and Ayrton Senna as drivers, the team delivered 11 straight wins. The rest of the field was never really involved. The best was Gerhard Berger in his Ferrari, but the rest were nowhere. It was Ron Dennis's dream to win all 16 of the races. To achieve the perfect clean sweep and you would have been mad to bet against that. We think of it now as having been a golden age, but the truth is that the races were rather dull, much more so than they are today, when everyone is much closer, even if Mercedes has had an advantage.

Nothing seemed to work. In the first week of June Pope John Paul II visited Maranello and was taken for a spin around the Fiorano test track by Piero Ferrari. The Pope blessed the F1 cars and Italians hoped this would make a difference, but they both retired with mechanical failure a week later in Canada. The Pope's visit to Maranello did highlight the fact that Enzo Ferrari was not very well. He was then 90 years old and had been ailing for some months. The fact that he did not make it to the factory to see the Pope highlighted that things were very serious. In the course of July, the reports got worse. And then on Sunday, August 14 it was announced that Il Commendatore had "serenely ended his earthly life". He was interred in the family tomb in the San Cataldo Cimitero in Modena.

Two weeks later, it was a sombre F1 circus which gathered in Spa. It was the same old story. McLaren dominated. Both Ferraris retired. A fortnight later they reconvened at Monza. It was the same story again. The McLarens qualified side by side on the front row. The Ferraris were third and fourth. The order did not change at the start and remained a McLaren 1-2 until lap 35 when Prost retired with an engine failure. Senna stayed ahead, working his way through the midfield, lapping them one by one. At the start of the 50th lap (in a 51 lap race), Senna came up behind the Williams of Jean-Louis Schlesser, who was standing in for Nigel Mansell, who was out of action because of chicken pox. It was Schlesser's first F1 World Championship race and he was running a very decent 11th, three places behind his team-mate Riccardo Patrese. He saw Senna coming and tried to get out of the way. Senna went for the gap, but he had left Schlesser with nowhere to go and the two cars collided. Senna spun. The crowd at Monza went berserk, not only was the McLaren out, but suddenly there was a Ferrari 1-2, on the team's home turf. There were memorable scenes of wild celebration and as F1 cowered inside the paddock walls as the fans beseiged the compound, more than a few folk wondered if Enzo Ferrari, sitting on a cloud somewhere, might have been responsible... It was the only non-McLaren victory of the year.

Oh, lucky man...

Being in the right place at the right time is key to success in a Formula 1. One might complain that a driver did not deserve the success he had, but that's the way it is, the way the cards are dealt, and the way the dice fall.

In motor racing many believe that you make your own luck by being in the right place, being prepared and always doing a good job. As we saw in 2017, Valtteri Bottas was in the right place at the right time. Now he must deliver. The best example in F1 of being in the right place at the right time is probably Giancarlo Baghetti, who won the first three F1 races he entered.

Born on Christmas Day in 1934, Baghetti was both fortunate and unfortunate at birth. It meant that he would be given fewer presents throughout this lifetime, as everyone combine their Christmas and birthday gifts, but at the same time his family owned a foundry – Stabilimenti Metallurgici Accorsi e Baghetti – which was based in Lecco, in the beautiful lakeland to the north of Milan. This was a business big enough to have its own football team, and it meant that Giancarlo and his brother Marco did not struggle for money.

Giancarlo always wanted to be a racing driver, but he was worried about his father's reaction to the idea and so raced secretly, borrowing his father's car, which was tuned by night by Angelo Dagrada, a local garage owner and borrowed for weekends, ostensibly so the boys could spectate at events. His first race was the Coppa della Madunina at Monza in 1956 and his adventures expanded the following year with events such as the Trieste-Opicina and Coppa del Cimino hillclimbs and the Coppa Carri at Monza. There was a similar programme in 1958 with the primary exception being that the Baghetti brothers entered the Mille Miglia. The classic event had been banned the previous year, but there was a gruelling 32-hour 1,593 km trial through the mountain roads of northern Italy, with seven timed stages along the way. There were 111 entries and the Baghetti brothers were second in class and seventh overall.

This led to a friend, Mario Poltronieri, a racer who went on to become a celebrated TV commentator, mentioning Baghetti to Carlo Abarth as someone to look out for. Abarth signed Baghetti to race for him in 1959. This was quite successful and in 1960 Baghetti tried single seaters, driving a Formula Junior built by his friend Dagrada. This too was a great success. At the end of the year Giancarlo received a phone call from Eugenio Dragoni, who ran Scuderia Ambroeus, and was also team manager at Ferrari. Dragoni took Baghetti to meet Enzo Ferrari and, much to Giancarlo's surprise, he was offered a Ferrari contract. He tested a sports car soon afterwards and was sufficiently fast for Ferrari to decide to enter him for the 1961 Sebring 12 Hours, as team-mate to Willy Mairesse. The car would be taken over by Wolfgang Von Trips and Richie Ginther in the course of the race, but they would all be listed as having finished second.

Ferrari was keen to promote an Italian in F1 and agreed to loan a Ferrari 156 to Scuderia Ambroeus for the Gran Premio di Siracusa on April 25 and the Gran Premio di Napoli at Posillipo on May 14. Despite strong opposition at Syracuse, Baghetti used the Ferrari horsepower to good effect and beat all the big names from Porsche, Cooper, Lotus and BRM. Two weeks later, with most of the stars racing at Monaco, he won at Posillipo as well. Two F1 races. Two wins.

Ferrari had expanded to four cars for the Belgian GP with local hero Olivier Gendebien driving alongside the regular stars Wolfgang Von Trips, Phil Hill and Richie Ginther, and Enzo Ferrari decided to send a fourth car to Reims as well, to try Baghetti in a World Championship race. Hill, Von Trips and Ginther qualified 1-2-3, with Baghetti 12th, five seconds slower than pole position.

Hill led from the start with Ginther and Von Trips chasing as Baghetti worked his way up the order. Von Trips then stopped with engine trouble on the 18th lap, Hill led for 20 laps then spun and stalled and was a lap behind. Ginther led for three laps and then his engine failed. This left Dan Gurney's Porsche fighting Baghetti, they changed places a number of times but on the last lap Baghetti pulled out of Gurney's slipstream and took the lead a couple of hundred yards before the finish line to become the first and, to date, only man to win on his F1 World Championship debut.

He raced twice more that year but failed to repeat his success and in 1962 Ferrari had lost its advantage. He raced four times and scored points three times but then decided to follow Hill and many of the Ferrari staff to join the ATS team. This was not a success and with the doors closed to him at Maranello, he could only find a two-year-old BRM entered by Scuderia Centro Sud in 1964. He enjoyed some success in other forms of racing and appeared at the Italian GP each year until 1967 but the machinery was never competitive.

He retired from racing in 1968, married Chichi Vianini and started a new career as an art photographer and later as a journalist. He became the editor of the weekly car magazine Auto Oggi in 1986, but died of cancer at the age of 60 in November 1995. His son Aaron is an art photographer now based in London.

Being in the right place, at the wrong time

In racing, one must grab the opportunities when they come along because they may be the only chance to show one's abilities. Very few get second chances.

One or two poor performances can blight a career, as we saw with Luca Badoer in 2009 when he replaced the injured Felipe Massa at Ferrari. Two poor races and he was gone, his career over.

In many ways, this is a similar story to that of Giancarlo Martini, an Italian, born near Ravenna, soon after the end of World War II. The family was not originally wealthy. His uncle Camillo was a pig farmer and in 1960 Giancarlo's brother Luciano bought his uncle's business and began expanding ambitiously, adding a delicatessen to the empire before deciding that there were better ways to make money. He began refining animal fats and then diversified into the manufacturing of vegetable oils, margarine, chocolate and chocolate substitutes. Further diversification led to ice cream and then a range of pastry products under the Master Martini brand – all on an industrial scale. Today the firm is known as Unigra and employs hundreds of people at a large plant in Conselice. It does business in 90 countries.

The success of Unigra would give the family financial stability, but much of it happened after Giancarlo needed money to go racing. He was not a passionate entrepreneur like his older brother. His dream was to be a racing driver and by the early 1970s, when he was in his mid-twenties, he had become a leading light in Formula Italia, the national championship before youngsters moved to the international scene.

In 1973 he was the title, driving for a two-year-old operation called Scuderia del Passatore, sponsored by the industrial rubber company Everest, and run by a young Giancarlo Minardi. Martini moved up to Formula 2 in 1974, driving a March-BMW for Pino Trivellato, but the following year Minardi arrived in F2 and so Martini rejoined him, using March-BMWs. They were not overly successful, but they were ambitious and that year Enzo Ferrari was talked into a plan to help develop young Italian talent by providing a 312T Formula 1 car for a customer team: Scuderia Everest.

Martini was then 28 and hardly a youngster, but this did not seem to matter that much. He was entered in two non-championship F1 races: the Daily Mail Race of Champions in March at Brands Hatch and the International Trophy at Silverstone in April. He qualified 15th out of 16 at Brands Hatch and then embarrassed himself by crashing in the warm-up, damaging the car beyond immediate repair. At Silverstone he qualified 10th out of 18, not far behind Mario Andretti's Lotus and Carlos Pace's Brabham, but then finished 10th in the race. It wasn't a bad effort, but it wasn't enough to create much excitement.

He disappeared back to Formula 2, where he finished seventh in the championship that year before switching to different machinery in 1977 when Minardi ran Martini in a Martini. By then younger Italian stars such as Riccardo Patrese and Elio de Angelis were rising. In 1978, Martini switched to the Aurora F1 series, a British-based series and driving an Ensign he finished fourth at Zandvoort and then won at Donington Park. After a couple more F2 races, he disappeared from the sport.

He would pop up again a few years later when his nephew, Luciano's son Pierluigi, began racing. He would be rather more successful than his uncle, winning the European Formula 3 title in 1983, finishing third in Formula 3000 and then heading into Formula 1 with Minardi. He would compete in 119 races with the team – but never finished better than fourth. His lack of language skills held him back, but in 1999 Pierluigi would win the Le Mans 24 Hours for BMW Motorsport, partnered by Joachim Winkelhock and Yannick Dalmas.

Giancarlo Martini died of cancer at the age of 66 in March 2013.

Chipping away at success

There are many great drivers in the world but not all can make it to Formula 1. You need to have the right connections and then your talent will – hopefully – do the rest. Sons of famous racing fathers have an advantage in this respect, although they are always greeted with scepticism until they prove themselves. Others come from wealthy backgrounds and their money eases their way through the sport. But some drivers have neither connections nor money – and have to make things happen…

Philip Toll Hill Jr was not by nature a combative character. He was born in Miami, his father then being a Mack Truck salesman and his mother a farm girl with musical ambitions. In 1926, soon after his mother discovered she was pregnant, Miami was hit by what has become known as the Great Miami Hurricane. Several hundred people were killed and 43,000 people were made homeless. There was looting and martial law was declared. The Hills waited until the baby came and then packed up their belongings and drove across the country to Los Angeles, where they settled in the pleasant seaside resort of Santa Monica, not far from Hollywood, the film-making capital of the world. Hill was an entrepreneur and soon became a prominent local Democrat and by 1935 had been appointed the Postmaster of the city. His wife wrote hymns. Both drank a lot and Phil's childhood was not a happy one, except that his Aunt Helen, his mother's sister, doted on him and his brother and sister.

Helen Grasselli had previously been married to the owner of Cleveland's Grasselli Chemical Company (later to become part of the DuPont empire), who had no children of her own – and no shortage of money. Phil was a sickly child, clumsy and not good at sport. The only thing he was good at was identifying cars, and this would lead to a passion for all things automotive. He was sent to school in the Hollywood Military Academy, in nearby Brentwood, where his friends included a young George Hearst Jr, one of the grandchildren of media tycoon William Randolph Hearst. They shared an interest in cars and when Aunt Helen bought young Phil an old Model T Ford he and George, who owned a Model A Ford, would race the cars on the estate roads on the Hearst ranch in Santa Monica Canyon, which included a quarter mile dirt oval (for horses), which the boys used as a racetrack. He learned the mechanics of cars from Aunt Helen's chauffeur Louis.

He was turned down by the US Army because of sinus troubles, but worked in the nearby Douglas Aircraft factory, assembling nose-guns for a while, before enrolling to study business at UCLA. It was not what he wanted and he dropped out and went to work for the recently-estabished International Motors on Wilshire Boulevard in Hollywood, where many film stars went to buy imported sports cars. In the evenings he worked with a midget racing team and indulged in a fair amount of street racing, which was prevalent at the time. He took part in his first rally in 1948 and then the midget driver with whom he worked broke his leg and so the team owner told Hill to race instead. This was not a great success, but Hill's passion was undimmed.

He convinced the owner of International Motors to send him to Britain to learn about the cars he was selling and in the autumn of 1949 Phil sailed from Boston to Southampton to spend the winter months on secondment with Jaguar, Rolls Royce and MG. On Saturday May 13, 1950, he went to Silverstone to watch the British Grand Prix, the first ever round of the new FIA Formula 1 World Championship. Four days later he sailed from Southampton, bound for New York on the RMS Queen Mary, taking with him a Jaguar XK120 sports car, which he had bought. He drove the car 700 miles from New York to Indianapolis and watched the Indy 500 on May 30, becoming probably the only spectator to see both of the first two World Championship events. And then he motored the 2,000 miles from there home to California.

Later in the year, with a pit crew consisting of a gawky 20-year-old car enthusiast called Richie Ginther and George Hearst Jr, Phil won the Pebble Beach Cup, driving from the back of the field to victory. His victory put him on the racing map.

His parents both died early in 1951, which was a relief for Hill – and he spent his inheritance buying a Ferrari from Luigi Chinetti. This led to a Ferrari drive on the 1952 Carrera Panamerica. The constant deaths in racing in that era weighed heavily on Hill and he quit racing for a while and worked as a mechanic again before being drawn back into the sport when working on a Darryl Zanuck movie called *The Racers* in 1954, starring Kirk Douglas. He prepared the cars involved and did some of the stunt driving and started racing again when the film was finished. In 1955 he finished second in the Sebring 12 Hours, with Carroll Shelby, prompting Chinetti to offer him a Ferrari factory drive at Le Mans, alongside Umberto Maglioli. He joined Ferrari as a factory sports car driver in 1956 and began a successful career which included Le Mans victories for the company in 1958, 1961 and 1962.

In 1958, frustrated at not being given a chance in Formula 1, he decided to rent Jo Bonnier's Maserati 250F for the French GP, where Ferrari driver Luigi Musso was killed. Hill finished seventh. A month later he joined Ferrari for the German GP, the race in which Peter Collins was killed. He then became a fulltime Ferrari F1 driver. He scored his first podiums with third that year at Monza and in Morocco. There were three more podiums in 1959 and in 1960 he was joined in the team by Ginther, his former mechanic. That year Phil won his first F1 victory at Monza. And in 1961 he won the title…

What could have been?

Before Andretti, Phil Hill and Dan Gurney, American F1 drivers who raced in Europe tended to be wealthy young amateurs. They were adventurers who were often New England types, educated at Harvard, Princeton or Yale, or the kids of wealthy folk who lived in France. Most made little impression. Herbert MacKay-Fraser was a little the same, but at the same time quite different.

He was a slightly mysterious figure. You can find different dates and places of birth for him and his name is odd because his father was simply Fraser and his mother was not a MacKay. So his name was not really his name. Government records are government records, so one can say with certainty that Herbert Fraser was born in Recife in Brazil in 1922 – not in Connecticut in 1927.

His father is often said to have been the owner of a coffee plantation, but in truth he was a bank manager – although he did acquire a plantation, which boosted the family coffers considerably. Herbert Cecil Fitzroy Fraser had been born a British citizen, on the island of Saint Vincent in the British West Indies. As the name suggests, he was the son of a Scottish emigrant. He moved to New York in 1904 and joined the National City Bank on Wall Street as a teller. He became a U.S. citizen in 1917 and after the war he married an American, seven years his junior. Soon afterwards the couple went to live in Buenos Aires, where the bank wanted him to go to manage its local interests. After that it was on to Recife, where Herbert Jr was born in 1922. Four years later, Herbert Sr switched to become the manager of the Royal Bank of Canada in Rio de Janeiro.

With the bank salary and a coffee plantation, money was not a problem, but Herbert Sr did not live to enjoy it. He died unexpectedly, at the age of just 46, in the middle of 1933. His widow Grace liked Brazil and stayed on, but Herbert Jr, who was then 11, was soon sent off to boarding school in New Hampshire. When the war came, he enlisted, but it was too late for him to see any active service. When peace returned, he tried his hand at ranching in Wyoming, spent a lot of time skiing in Idaho and then drifted into real estate.

He did not discover car racing until he was 31, when the West Coast sports car craze was just kicking off. He made his racing debut at the end of 1953, in a race in Reno, at the wheel of a Jaguar XK120. The following year he raced in both California and in Brazil, and by the summer of 1955 he had relocated to London, where he drove around in a Ferrari (a rare thing in those days) and hung out with Jo Bonnier.

He shared a Lotus at Le Mans with Colin Chapman and built a reputation as an able racer. He then moved to a small Italian village called Bonassola on the coast between Genoa and La Spezia, where he lived with his new wife Marga and their baby daughter. He had two other children, living in Idaho.

In the summer of 1957, BRM offered him a chance in F1 for the French GP at Rouen. Roy Salvadori had moved to Vanwall because Stirling Moss and Tony Brooks were both out of action: Moss with a sinus infection and Brooks as a result of a crash at Le Mans. MacKay-Fraser did a good job, running sixth behind the Maseratis and the Lancia-Ferraris until his transmission failed. It was a promising F1 debut and it seemed he was bound for a future in Grand Prix racing.

A week later he was entered for the Grand Prix de Reims in a Maserati, and qualified well. He was also entered for the Coupe Internationale de Vitesse Formula 2 race in a factory Lotus 11 sports car, which had been stripped down for F2. He was going well until, for reasons unknown, he arrived far too fast in the first corner. The car ran out of road and went on to the grass for about 60 metres before it ran over a low earth bank and rolled. Drivers then preferred not to wear seat belts and so MacKay-Fraser was thrown out and suffered serious injuries on landing. A helicopter was on hand to fly him to hospital in Reims, but it was too late. He died during the flight. We will never know how good he might have been. He was buried a week later in the local cemetery at Bezannes. Although soon forgotten by the F1 world, he was the first Lotus driver to die in one of the factory cars. No great epitaph.

When Worldwide Racing won a Grand Prix

People say that Team Lotus won 74 victories, but if you look closely at the paperwork, you will see that this was not actually the case. Team Lotus won 73 times and Worldwide Racing won the Italian Grand Prix in 1972, with Emerson Fittipaldi driving a Lotus-Cosworth 72D. It was the second year that Worldwide Racing had been seen at Monza and it was clearly Team Lotus, but entered under a different name. This was deemed to be necessary because Team Lotus and its designers Colin Chapman and Maurice Philippe were at the time under investigation by Italian magistrates over the accident in 1970 that had killed Jochen Rindt. Italian law has what is known as omicidio colposo, which is the action of causing the death of a person without intention. This carries with it a possible prison sentence of between six months and five years if the accused is found guilty.

After Rindt's death Italian magistrates opened an investigation into the accident. This would ultimately conclude that the accident was caused by the failure of a right front brake shaft when it was under load. This resulted in Rindt losing control of the car, which slew to the left and crashed into the track-side barriers. These were not correctly secured and ultimately the official cause of Rindt's death was deemed to be the safety fence. However, the investigation took a great deal of time to reach any conclusions and Lotus was given legal advice to stay away from Italy until the outcome was known, just in case the Italian magistrates decided to issue arrest warrants. Thus, in September 1971 Worldwide Racing appeared at Monza, and Colin Chapman took the weekend off. There was only one car that year, a Lotus-Pratt & Whitney 56B turbine, driven by Emerson Fittipaldi, carrying the number 5. A year later Fittipaldi appeared ago in the Worldwide Racing Lotus (this time a Cosworth-engined 72D) and he won the race.

It was only in May 1973 that Magistrate Luigi Recupero, the Procuratore della Repubblica (the state prosecutor) of the Tribunale di Monza issued charges, saying that Chapman and the team were to blame because of the technical failure. However, it was agreed that Chapman would not be arrested if he visited Italy and the team's assets would not be seized and so in 1973 Team Lotus returned to being Team Lotus again. In the end, Chapman and Lotus were cleared of all charges in a trial that took place in 1976.

Where F1 in banned

Italy may have some troublesome laws when it comes to motor racing, but it is still a lot better than Switzerland, where Formula 1 race cannot take place.

Switzerland is a place where quite a few F1 drivers choose to live. There are tax benefits, the people are respectful and everything works. The country is one of only three that has a Formula 1 team based on its soil (although Haas might argue that). The FIA is officially based in Paris, but a lot of the federation's activity is run from offices in Geneva.

The country has produced some very talented and successful drivers, notably Clay Regazzoni, Jo Siffert, Marc Surer, Sebastien Buemi, not to mention Romain Grosjean, who is half-Swiss and half-French. Switzerland won the A1GP World Cup of Motorsport in 2007-08, while Marcel Fässler has won the World Endurance Championship and is a three-time Le Mans winner. Neel Jani is also a WEC champion and Le Mans winner, while Fabio Leimer won the GP2 title a few years ago. It is a hotbed of motorsport activity – and yet motor racing is banned in Switzerland...

It was not always the case. Switzerland hosted its first Grand Prix in 1934 and for many years it was one of the highlights of the Grand Prix calendar, with the races taking place on the spectacular Bremgarten circuit, in the forests just outside the city of Berne. The track consisted of one sweeping curve after another, with trees all around, different road surfaces and, often, poor weather. It was considered one of the great racing circuits.

When the Formula 1 World Championship began in 1950, Bremgarten was the third race in Europe, following Silverstone and Monaco.

The Le Mans disaster in 1955, in which more than 80 people were killed after Pierre Levegh's Mercedes ran into the back of Lance Macklin's Austin Healey and was launched into the crowd, led to the laws being changed in many countries.

The Swiss introduced the Loi Fédérale sur la Circulation Routière in 1959. Article 52 of this states that motor racing is banned. There can be hillclimbs and slaloms, as cars are not racing one another, but rather against the clock.

In the 1960s there were some major hillclimb events, notably Ollon-Villars and

Sierra Montana-Crans, which hosted what was known as the Swiss Mountain Grand Prix, but the law forced the Swiss racing fraternity to organize circuit races in neighbouring countries. In 1982 there was even a Swiss Grand Prix, run on the Dijon-Prenois circuit, although this was really only a ruse to allow France to have an additional race that year. The event was won by Keke Rosberg in a Williams, the only victory he scored in his World Championship year.

In the last 15 years, there have been several discussions about whether the ban should be lifted, but many Swiss people are deeply conservative. There was considerable resistance to motor racing even before the Le Mans accident, specifically related to the holding of races on Sundays. The power of religion is waning, with adherence to churches having declined from close to 95 percent in 1980 to about 7o percent today. But now environmental questions are central to the discussion, although the Swiss own more cars per capita than many other European countries, including Britain. In 2009 a motion was passed in the Swiss Lower House, known as the Nationalrat, to allow racing, but it was defeated in the Upper House, known as the Ständerat.

In March 2015, however, the law was modified to allow Formula E, although the electric car racers will still have to abide by a maximum average speed set by whichever canton holds a race.

Some of the roads which made up the Bremgarten circuit are still there, but much has disappeared beneath urban development. Amazingly, however, there is one permanent Swiss racing facility, a tiny circuit called Lignieres, on a mountain plateau in the Jura, near Neufchatel. This was built in 1961 in the hope that the government would change its attitude to racing. Today it is owned by the Touring Club Suisse and is used for driver training.

Wouldn't it be nice to have some racing in the country…

What's wrong with F1?

It is a strange irony that the automobile club that ran the very first Grand Prix is today implacably opposed to getting involved in the FIA Formula 1 World Championship. It was 111 years ago, in the early part of 1906 that the Automobile Club de la Sarthe was founded in the city of Le Mans. This group of racing fans went quickly into action, hosting the very first Grand Prix de l'Automobile Club de France a little over five months later. Even with the help of the ACF this was an impressive achievement. The event was designed to replace the ACF's Gordon Bennett Cup, which had been the biggest international motor racing event of the year since 1900. A circuit was laid out on country roads to the east of Le Mans, running from the start-finish area near the village of Champagné, just outside Le Mans, towards the city and then going into hairpin and heading off east, down to Saint-Calais, where it turned north to Vibraye and La Ferté-Bernard, where it headed south-west back to Le Mans. It was 65 miles in length.

Grand Prix racing did not return to city until 1921, by which time club been renamed the Automobile Club de l'Ouest. There was a new road circuit was laid out to the south of the city, running from the suburbs down the RN138 to the village of Mulsanne and then turning to the west and returned to Le Mans through the forests close to the village of Arnage. This would become the basis of the circuit used for the 24 Hours of Le Mans, which was held for the first time in 1923. The Grand Prix de l'ACF returned to Le Mans in 1929, being won by a Bugatti, but after that the race settled at the Montlhéry autodrome near Paris and then on the magnificent road circuits at Reims and Rouen.

The problem with road circuits is that they cost a lot of money to prepare and generate nothing between the big events. By the 1950s, the idea of having a permanent racing circuit at Le Mans, in order for the track facilities to be used more efficiently, with a racing school and for industry testing, was a sensible one. To the south of the pits and grandstand area was a great deal of land, much of it was sandy and pine-covered and so expanding the facilities was relatively simply. The project called for the pits, grandstands and the paddock, plus the start-finish straight, to be integrated into a new circuit behind the paddock. The project was supported by ACO President Jean-Marie Lelièvre, its managing-director Raymond Acat and the head of its competition committee Pierre Allanet. Charles de Cortanze (a member of a famous racing family) was also involved as was Charles Deutsch, a civil engineer with the French government's Corps des Ponts et Chaussées, who designed the track, when he was not running his own sports car firm called Deutsch et Bonnet (DB).

Deutsch's new circuit split from the main track just after the Dunlop Bridge with a curling right-hander that sent the cars back towards the paddock. This was followed by a long curling left-hander which went up to a double right set of corners which led on to the back straight, which headed back towards the paddock, kinking left when it arrived there and then going through some tight corners before rejoining the main circuit just before the pits. The construction work was completed in 1965 and the track was opened, being named after the great Ettore Bugatti.

Two years later, the French Grand Prix returned to Le Mans to try the Bugatti Circuit. The event took place on the weekend between two Formula 2 races, the Grand Prix de Reims and the Grand Prix de Rouen-les-Essarts. Thus the racers arrived from Reims and found that the Bugatti track had none of the grandeur of where they had been, nor where they were going. They were not impressed. It did not help that there were only 20,000 spectators (which meant that the ACO probably took a big financial hit). The fans who did attend saw Graham Hill in the new Lotus-Cosworth 49 leading the field away, before Jack

Brabham got ahead of him in the Brabham-Repco. Jim Clark then passed both and Hill overtook Brabham and so it was a Lotus 1-2 until both Hill and Clark both suffered transmission failures, leaving Brabham ahead again. Second-placed Dan Gurney retired his Eagle-Weslake and Denny Hulme in the second Brabham-Repco passed Chris Amon's Ferrari and so it ended up being a Brabham-Repco 1-2 with Amon third.

The only Frenchman in the field was Guy Ligier in a Cooper-Maserati, but he was not classified, having finished several laps down on the winners.

The Grand Prix never returned. Le Mans stuck with its 24 Hour race and ran the Motorcycle GP on an irregular basis thereafter until 2000, when it became the race's permanent home.

But whenever Formula 1 is mentioned, the ACO firmly says no. A strange thing given that it is within easy reach of Paris and could draw a big crowd...

The big one

The most prestigious race on the Formula 1 calendar is, without question, the Monaco Grand Prix. It is seen as being essential to the sport, part of its brand. The race is run by the Automobile Club de Monaco, which began life in 1890 as a cycling club with just 21 members, known as Sport Vélocipédique Monégasque (SVM).

In 1907 its President Henri Tairraz convinced the other members to change the name to Sport Automobile et Vélocipédique de Monaco (SAVM), as the automobile was rapidly becoming popular amongst the wealthy gentlemen of the Principality. Two years after this, in 1909, Alexandre Noghès took over as President. He was descended from a Spanish soldier who had become the commander of the Monaco garrison in 1820. By then the family had much influence and Noghès was the man in charge of public finances. He believed that Monaco would benefit financially from a major event in the winter months and, as automobiles were new and exciting, he proposed holding a Rallye Monte Carlo, which would see competitors start in various different cities around Europe and converge on Monte Carlo, with the winner being decided on the elegance of his car and the state it was in when it arrived. Much of the legwork organising the event in January 1911 was done by Noghès's son Antony, who was then 20 years of age. This was a tremendous success and over time, there developed a number of events which took place after the arrival of the cars, including some hillclimbs, notably to La Turbie and Mont Agel.

In 1925 when Alexandre proposed changing the name of the club to the Automobile Club de Monaco, as cycling had by then faded away and Antony, who had become the man in charge of Monaco's tobacco monopoly, as the Agent Général à la Régie des Tabacs et Allumettes, was sent to Paris to negotiate membership of the Association Internationale des Automobiles Clubs Reconnus (AIACR), the international governing body of motorsport, the forerunner of the FIA. The goal was to upgrade the ACM's status from being a regional French club to becoming a national sporting authority.

The AIACR rejected the proposal because the ACM did not host a single event on its own territory. Being the smallest sovereign state in the world apart from the Vatican, Monaco did not have much space to do anything, and the roads were not suited to competition. The furious young Noghès decided that this problem could be solved and proposed to hold a Grand Prix around the streets. It was a very radical idea at the time.

"They have the most astounding audacity in some parts of Europe," wrote The Autocar in England, when word of the idea arrived. It was, the magazine concluded, an unlikely event in a Principality "which does not possess a single open road of any length, but has only ledges on the face of a cliff". The French media was only slightly less dismissive, La Vie Automobile noting that this would be the first race in the heart of a city, but that "it goes without saying that the track is made up entirely of bends, steep uphill climbs and fast downhill runs".

Based on the proposal, the AIACR admitted the ACM to its membership in October 1928 and six months later, on April 14 1929, His Serene Highness Prince Pierre of Monaco formally opened the Monaco circuit, touring the track in a Voisin. The first race was a huge success and quickly became a key Grand Prix.

In 1940 Antony succeeded his father as President of the ACM. In 1979 the last corner of the circuit, formerly known as Gazometer, was renamed Virage Antony Noghès in his honour.

A strange event in Monaco...

Monaco is a difficult Grand Prix at the best of times, and it can be treacherous in the wet. The barriers are close at hand, there is no room for error. In the spring the weather on the French Riviera is usually very pleasant and that was certainly the case on Sunday, May 31, 1981, with the Principality bathed in sunshine. The bad news was that the start of the Monaco Grand Prix had to be delayed by an hour - because it was raining in the tunnel!

The problem was that there had been a fire in the kitchens of what was then called the Loews Hotel. The local fire brigade rushed to the scene and pumped hundreds of gallons of water into the kitchens. This found its way through the floors and there was "rain" in the tunnel.

You couldn't make this stuff up...

Allez Les Bleus!

The second Monaco Grand Prix in Monaco was won by Frenchman René Dreyfus, at the wheel of a Bugatti. It was a cause for great celebration for the French - a Frenchman had won the race, driving a French car. Allez les bleus!

Four years later they played La Marseillaise for Guy Moll, but he was driving an Italian Alfa Romeo. It was 21 years before they played La Marseillaise again for Maurice Trintignant's triumph in 1953, in a Ferrari. Trintignant's would win again 1958, this time in a British-built Cooper.

In 1972 the first of a new generation of French racing stars, Jean-Pierre Beltoise, won the race, driving a British BRM. Six years later his protégé Patrick Depailler won in a Tyrrell. Of that celebrated generation of French racing stars only one - Alain Prost - won Monaco, and he did it four times, in a British-built McLaren. His last win was in 1988. The number of Frenchmen on the grid thinned out and by 1996 only two were left: Jean Alesi (31) and Olivier Panis (29). Alesi seemed the more likely to win races in his Benetton, while Panis's Ligier-Mugen was not a bad car, but didn't look like winner. When the F1 circus arrived in Monaco "Olive" had one point to his name and he qualified 14th on the grid. Traditionally there is never much overtaking at Monaco and so there was no chance that he was going to win. But it was an odd day, with overcast conditions with occasional showers. Things started strangely with what seemed to be two Michael Schumachers on the grid: one driving a Ferrari, the other in a McLaren, Michael having loaned David Coulthard a helmet because the Scotsman was having misting up problems with his. Michael made a poor start from pole in his Ferrari and so Damon Hill took the lead for Williams. Further back Jos Verstappen, who had gambled on slicks, went sailing into the wall at Sainte-Dévote, after a bump with Mika Hakkinen's McLaren. The two Minardis also collided, taking out Pedro Lamy and Giancarlo Fisichella. At the top of the hill, Michael Schumacher tapped a kerb and slid into the wall. He was out. At Rascasse Rubens Barrichello crashed his Jordan-Peugeot. This meant that by the of the lap Hill had a monster lead of 4.3secs over the Benettons of Gerhard Berger and Alesi, although Berger disappeared with gearbox failure after 10 laps, by which time Hill's lead was more than 10secs. After 28 laps he pitted and emerged from the pits around 30secs clear of Alesi. Then Damon's engine blew... Jean was the leader. Allez Les Bleues!

Next up was Panis who had jumped to fourth during the pit stops and then finding himself behind the Ferrari of Eddie Irvine, he bullied his way through. He had chased after Alesi but then spun on Hill's oil and dropped further behind Alesi. Still, it was a French 1-2 until the Benetton suddenly started handling so strangely that even Jean wasn't brave enough to drive it. He headed for the pits. The rear suspension had broken. Panis was in the lead. Coulthard, disguised as Schumacher, chased him while Johnny Herbert found himself third. He had overtaken no-one all day, but had simply stayed off the walls in his Sauber. The only other finisher was Heinz-Harald Frentzen in the second Sauber, a lap down after putting after a collision with Irvine's Ferrari. No one else was running after Irvine spun and took out Mikas Hakkinen and Salo a few laps from the finish.

France had its second victory for a French driver in a French car and F1 had equalled its record for the fewest finishers in a race.

Sometimes winning is not easy

The desire to win races is something that shines through when you talk to F1 drivers. They all want to win. Being second is losing. And yet, there is one famous Grand Prix when no-one seemed able to win.

The Monaco Grand Prix of 1982 was so strange that if one wrote it as fiction, no-one would think it credible. It was, plain and simple, unbelievable.

The race meeting began only 10 days after the death of Gilles Villeneuve in qualifying for the Belgian GP at Zolder and Ferrari was still in a state of shock and arrived in Monaco with just one car, for Didier Pironi. In qualifying that year René Arnoux lapped the track in 1m23.281s, just over half a second faster than Riccardo Patrese's Brabham-Cosworth, with Bruno Giacomelli's V12 Alfa Romeo two-tenths behind, with Alain Prost fourth in the second Renault turbo and Pironi fifth in the turbocharged Ferrari 126C2, with Keke Rosberg sixth in his Cosworth-powered Williams FW08.

The start at Monaco is often messy but in 1982 it was neat and tidy with Arnoux leading Giacomelli, Patrese and a slow-starting Prost. Alain quickly overtook the Brabham and when Giacomelli retired after just four laps with an axle problem, Prost was second and Renault had a 1-2. They were chinking glasses in the Renault hospitality until the 15th lap when Arnoux spun and stalled. Prost moved ahead with Patrese chasing him, keeping up the pressure. It was fairly stable race after that until rain began to fall lightly on the circuit in the last 12 laps of the race. Rosberg hit a barrier on lap 65 and his team-mate Derek Daly did similarly but managed to keep going, minus his rear wing, part of his front wing and leaking oil from a damaged gearbox.

Two laps from home Prost came through the chicane, the car snapped to the right and ploughed into the barrier, bouncing back across the track for a second impact before coming to rest back on the inside of the track. He hobbled away, having banged his legs inside the cockpit. Patrese, who had never won a race, came through into the lead, with two and a half laps to go. How could it possibly go wrong?

He set off on the last lap but as he headed down into the Loews Hairpin,the car slid sideways, spun around and stalled. The TV commentators were bouncing off the walls as well as Pironi took the lead, the Ferrari missing its nosecone. Also seemed to be well until he arrived at Tabac where a gaggle of lapped cars caught him and all went past before Sainte-Dévote. The Ferrari seemed slow as it climbed the hill, but it was still about 10 seconds clear of Andrea de Cesaris's Alfa Romeo. As the Ferrari came down the hill from Loews it was slower than ever. In fact, it was coasting. It was out of fuel and Pironi parked it in the tunnel.

The lead should then have gone to de Cesaris, but when the TV cameras found the Alfa Romeo it was stopped beside the track at the top of the hill, having run out of fuel as well. The driver was distraught. Everyone scrambled to figure out who was next. The TV cameras zoomed in on Daly just as he climbed from the battered Williams, his gearbox having died just before Tabac. This meant that the two Lotuses, two laps down, would finish 1-2 - if they could make it to the finish line. Elio de Angelis was leading at that point, but would be overtaken in those confused final minutes by Nigel Mansell.

This was overlooked by many as Patrese suddenly appeared at the final corner and took the chequered flag. His Brabham had been pointing out into the road in the middle of the Loews Hairpin and the marshals arrived and pushed the Brabham to get it out of the way. It was downhill from there and Patrese realised that he might be able to bump-start the stalled car. It worked but he was beside himself, thinking he had thrown away his first F1 victory.

He did not see Pironi's car parked in the tunnel. He had no idea he had won the race. Mansell and de Angelis eventually came round but they had finished only 74 laps, whereas Pironi and de Cesaris had each done 75. So the Ferrari driver was classified second, with de Cesaris third, Mansell fourth and de Angelis fifth. Daly was given sixth.

A race without a route

The current Formula 1 tyre supplier, Pirelli, has been owned since June last year by the China National Chemical Corporation, known as ChemChina, a state-owned enterprise, based in Beijing. This may seem a little odd for a celebrated Italian enterprise, but from a motorsport point of view, it is apt.

Pirelli's first success in motorsport was an adventure which began in the Chinese capital: the Peking-Paris race of 1907.

The idea of such an extraordinary challenge came from the French newspaper Le Matin, which announced in January that year, that it would promote the race, starting in June, to prove the power of the new-fangled automobiles. The prize would be a single bottle of champagne. The cantankerous Autocar in England dismissed the idea as "one of those hardy annuals that crop up when there is nothing else to talk about in the automobile world" and dismissed the whole affair as self-promotion.

There were 62 expressions of interest, which became 40 entries, but there was little time and only five cars appeared in Peking. There were no rules beyond the fact that the cars had to be driven. There was no route, mainly because there were no roads. It was 9,300 miles of do-it-yourself adventure. The plan was simple. The racers would follow the telegraph lines across the Gobi Desert and then run close to the Trans-Siberian railway. This would provide guidance and suitable stopping off points so the competitors could access the telegraph, so that the story could be told.

The Marquis Albert de Dion, owner of the De Dion Bouton automobile company, sent two of his cars to China by ship, while the crews went by train, organising fuel supplies along the route, something which involved sending a camel train into the Gobi Desert to create fuel dumps. They were also supposed to get authorisation for the event from the Chinese government, but they were not very successful in this respect. The racers did not care. They were going to set off whether the government liked it or not. The two de Dions were joined by a Dutch Spyker, a lightweight three-wheeler called a Contal and a hefty-looking Itala. The De Dions were to running on Dunlop tyres, the Spyker had Michelins and the Itala was on Pirellis. The Italian firm had only been making automobile tyres for seven years and the company founder's second son Alberto, then in his early twenties, was enthusiastic about the Peking-Paris to promote the products.

It helped, of course, that the Itala was driven by a full-blown Prince. Luigi Scipione Borghese, the 10th Prince of Sulmona, who was accompanied by his chauffeur Ettore Guizzardi. The 35-year-old Prince was the son of an Italian father and a Hungarian Countess. He had climbed mountains and had travelled cross-country from Beirut to the Pacific and had written several books about his adventures. He was also a member of the Italian Parliament. He was cool, calm and aristocratic. Guizzardi (25) was the son of a train driver who had joined the Prince's staff after a train crash close to the Borghese family castle in 1897, when he was 16. His father had been killed in the accident and Borghese took Guizzardi in and organised for him to be trained as a mechanic with Fiat and Ansaldo. The third crew member was a 33-year-old journalist Luigi Barzini, a war correspondent who was familiar with China, having covered the Boxer Rebellion and the Russo-Japanese War for Corriere della Sera. He was to report on the event for his newspaper and the Daily Telegraph.

The Itala was specially-built with a truck chassis, fitted with a detuned seven-litre Itala Grand Prix engine, and very basic bodywork, with planks of wood being used for mudguards (a brilliant idea, as it turned out). It had two seats in the front and one at the rear, the fourth seat having been replaced by two large fuel tanks.

A French military band played as the cars departed the French Embassy in Peking on June 10 and for the first few days, the cars remained in contact, meeting up each evening at refuelling stops. Borghese felt he was being held back and eventually lost patience and so went ahead on his own. The crew would have a series of adventures including being stuck in a marsh, which required rescue by a large number of oxen. The telegraph stations added interest as at one they found the operator drugged with opium and at another the operator explained that he had not sent a message in his entire six year stay.

Once in Russia they used an old military road, which dated from the construction of the Trans Siberian Railway but had become rather overgrown in places and on which many of the wooden bridges were rotting away. The Prince's answer was to cross them as quickly as possible, before they fell apart. On one such occasion Guizzardi was driving tentatively across such a structure when it gave way beneath them, flipping the car over, throwing Barzini and the driver out and leaving the Prince hanging upside down, under the car.

Later they drove along the the railway lines, but this caused a near-miss with an express and a later wheel to collapse from the vibration. When they reached Moscow the Itala crew was so confident of victory that they diverted to St Petersburg before heading down the ever-improving roads to reach the Russo-German border on August 4. They had a complicated moment in Belgium when stopped for speeding, as the local policeman refused to believe that Borghese was an Italian Prince who had driven from Peking, which was not altogether surprising…

They arrived in Paris to claim their champagne on August 10. Barzini would later publish a book in 11 languages, called *From Beijing to Paris in 60 Days*. He would go on to move from journalism into politics and became a strong supporter of Benito Mussolini, a senator and a member of the Fascist government. He died destitute in 1947 after the fall of the regime.

Pirelli's first taste of competition was a huge success and the company would move on to Grand Prix racing, winning its first major victory with Georges Boillot's Peugeot in the GP de l'ACF at Amiens in 1913.

The history of Magny Cours

The private lives of French politicians are deemed to be sacrosanct. Public interest stops at the bedroom door and no-one in France ever argues that a leader's political judgment is called into question by the breaking of his marriage vows. Having mistresses seems to be expected in the French political classes. President François Mitterrand, President between 1981 and 1995, was very active in this respect, indeed there are some who believe that it was the President's complicated love life which resulted in the French Grand Prix moving to Magny-Cours in 1991. It was a scandal at the time, because the race was established at Paul Ricard and moving it to a circuit in the middle of nowhere, with no autoroute access, no infrastructure to support a race and insufficient hotels and restaurants. Why this happened is a story which goes back to 1946 when the 30-year-old Mitterrand, from a village near Cognac, in the west of France, was soundly beaten in an election in the suburbs of Paris. He was desperate to become a *deputé* (similar to an Member of Parliament). Mitterand and so asked Henri Queuille the leader of the Radical party, what he could do. He was told to go to Nevers, in the Nièvre department, 150 miles south of Paris on the River Loire, on the basis that there would be no real opposition.

Mitterand arrived two weeks before the election and toured the region building support. At the time local alliances decided many elections and Mitterand quickly convinced the right wing voters and the clergy to support him. His big breakthrough came when he landed the support of the local farming community. It was enough to get him elected and into the government of Paul Ramadier as Minister for War Veterans. Jean Bernigaud, a 26-year-old cattle farmer, played a key role in getting the local farmers so support Mitterand and the two men would remain friends thereafter. In the late 1950s, Mitterand became the godfather of Bernigaud's sixth child. His political power in the region grew after he became the mayor of Chateau-Chinon in 1959 and President du Conseil Général of the Nièvre in 1964. Bernigaud, for his part, became the mayor of Magny-Cours in 1957 and 10 years later joined the Conseil Général. Later, when he had become

President of France, Mitterand encouraged Pierre Bérégovoy to become the mayor of Nevers in 1983, and *deputé* for the department in 1986.

Bernigaud was a man who was keen to promote the region. As early as 1954, he went to Reims and saw the French Grand Prix and noted that this was held on public roads. He went home with the idea of having a racing circuit in the roads around his village. He was working on the idea when in 1955 the Le Mans disaster occurred and as a result safety rules were changed and a road circuit became impossible. Bernigaud decided to use a piece of his own land, known as the Domaine de Bardonnay, which was located close to the Route Nationale 7, next to the hamlet of Les Gaillères. The first circuit was for karts only and was 510 metres in length. It opened in May 1961 and was christened the Circuit Jean Behra, after the French racing star who had been killed at Avus in 1959. The circuit was extended in 1969 and then again in 1971, at which point it reached 2.4 miles in the length. Sadly, Bernigaud died that year, at the age of only 50, leaving his 48-year-old widow Jacqueline to run the farm. The management of the circuit was handed over to the ASA Nivernais.

Jacqueline was very close to Mitterand in this era and when he became President of France in 1981 he organized for her to became a consultant to the national oil company Elf, with a generous monthly fee. The problem was that the circuit was a huge drain on resources, but was very difficult to sell because of its remote location. It was the home of the celebrated École Winfield school and it hosted national events and an annual European Formula 3 event, but it was also getting older and requiring new investment. In 1986 Mitterand provided a solution to the problem. He convinced the Conseil Général, under Noël Berrier, who had been his vice-president on the Conseil since 1973, to buy the track for £1.5 million and then used public money to transform it into an international-level facility, capable of hosting F1 races. The project was supported by Mitterand's finance minister Beregovoy, who had become the mayor of Nevers in 1983, and was elected *deputé* for the Nièvre that year. The goal, in theory, was to create a motorsport industry cluster which would generate revenue for the region. Guy Ligier, another of Mitterand's buddies, moved his racing team from Vichy to the new circuit in 1989. The Fédération Française du Sport Automobile, under President Jean Marie Balestre, did not put up a fight and so F1 arrived in the summer of 1991.

The Grand Prix that went walkabout

The Australian GP is one of the oldest races to carry the title Grand Prix, although for much of its history it never had a proper home: it was the Walkabout Grand Prix, forever on the move, forever changing.

Italy has had a Grand Prix since 1921, Belgian since 1925 and Germany since 1926, but the first Australian GP was in 1928, a year before Monaco began.

Racing on the roads in Australia was forbidden, just as it was in Great Britain, but the Australians were a little less rigid and when the people of Phillip Island voted to create their own shire in 1927, it opened the way for racing on the island. The Victorian Motor Cycle Union and the Light Car Club of Victoria of Victoria proposed a race and the President of the shire's new council, Albert Sambell, a local land owner and entrepreneur, saw the benefit of the idea and the council voted to ignore the law and hold a race in March 1928. It was basically a club race on a 6.5-mile road circuit on dirt and gravel. In those days there was no bridge to the island so one had to go by ferry, but despite this 10,000 spectators arrived for the first event, a complicated handicap affair. It was won by Captain Arthur Waite, who had been wounded at Gallipoli and hospitalised. He soon met a young woman called Irene Austin and they were married and the gallant officer then began racing his father-in-law Herbert Austin's automobiles at Brooklands. He would later take his wife to Australia, where they established the first Austin dealership. The race was won in an Austin Seven.

The event stayed on Phillip Island until 1935, but remained a club event, won by local heroes with imported Bugattis, Rileys and MGs. There were some serious accidents and gradually pressure grew for change, although Phillip Island would later build a permanent circuit. The Australian GP, however, moved on, first to Victor Harbor, a seaside resort 30 miles south of Adelaide in South Australia and then on to a series of other road circuits, including an unsealed "Scenic Drive" at Mount Panorama in Bathurst (NSW) in 1938.

The race stopped during the war but was revived at Bathurst in 1947, the road having by then been surfaced and then it moved on to airfield circuits at Point Cook (Vic) and Leyburn (Qld) and road courses at Nuriootpa (SA) and Narrogin (WA). After another visit to Bathurst, the event moved to Albert Park in Melbourne in 1953 and 1956 and the first international drivers were invited to take part. The pattern of road and airfield courses continued with visits to Southport (Qld), Port Wakefield (SA) and Caversham (WA) before a return to Bathurst in 1958. The Tasmanians were keen to get involved as well and a fearsome road course was devised at Longford, but then it was on again to Lowood (Qld) and Mallala (SA). Lex Davison was the big winner in this era with four AGP victories.

By the 1960s, an increasing number of proper racing circuits emerged, including Warwick Farm, Sandown Park and Lakeside. The first AGP at 'The Farm' was in 1963 and was won by World Champion Jack Brabham and the race then became part of the Tasman Series, with visiting F1 stars taking on the locals during the European winter. The winners included Graham Hill, Jackie Stewart, Jim Clark and Chris Amon.

The F1 schedule was growing, however, and so the numbers of visitors reduced and Tasman turned to Formula 5000, with the likes of Frank Matich and Graham McRae being multiple winners of the event, but in the 1970s the growth of touring car racing pushed the single-seaters into the background. The Australian Drivers' Championship was run to Australian Formula 2 rules and the race was held at new circuits such as Oran Park (NSW) and Wanneroo (WA). Bob Jane, a celebrated racer and entrepreneur wanted to get in on the act with his Calder track near Melbourne and tried to host an F1 race in 1980. Alan Jones appeared in a Williams FW07 and an old Alfa was sent for Bruno Giacomelli while Didier Pironi was persuaded to take part in a locally-built Elfin. It was not a great success but Jane then opted for Formula Pacific rules in 1981 and paid F1 drivers to compete. These included Nelson Piquet, Jacques Lafitte and Alain Prost. They took on the best locals but the big winner in the era was Brazil's Roberto Moreno, who won three Australian GP victories. But by then plans were being laid for a World Championship F1 race in Adelaide – and the modern story of the Australian GP began on the streets of Adelaide in 1985. The race stayed for 11 years before moving to Albert Park 21 years ago.

Politics and racing circuits

Europe has had a long history of war – which is why the European Union was eventually invented. Wars result in countries winning and losing territory and so there are today all kinds of strange anomalies when it comes to frontiers.

The country known today as Belgium was often involved in the fighting as it had the misfortune to be a place where the French, German and Dutch borders meet. Not far from Antwerp, for example, one can find a complicated district consisting of Baarle-Hertog (which is Belgian) and Baarle-Nassau (which is Dutch). There are 22 Belgian exclaves inside Dutch territory and six Dutch exclaves inside the largest of the Belgian exclaves. You can cross the border several times simply by walking down the main street.

On the other side of Belgium, near Eupen, one can find several strips of Belgian land, just a few metres wide, that meander through Germany along the path of a railway line. These remained Belgian when the borders changed, in some places the tracks have been torn up, but the land remains Belgian...

Still, there is one good thing about all of this for motor racing fans, because without borders moving around, we would probably not have the Spa Francorchamps circuit.

The region to the east of Spa has long been a messy part of Europe. Parts of it belonged to Luxembourg, other bits to the Archbishop of Trier and some districts to the Holy Roman Empire. The whole region became French in 1795 but then, after the Congress of Vienna in 1815, most of it was ceded to the United Kingdom of the Netherlands, although the East Cantons (Eupen, Malmedy and St Vith) were given to Prussia. The Belgian Revolution in 1830 led to the southern part of the United Kingdom of the Netherlands breaking away to become Belgium.

Spa developed as a resort, where people visited to take the iron-rich waters. Eventually it became a little too popular for some and so a new hotel was built opposite the first station on the railway line towards Luxembourg. It was quiet but allowed easy access to Spa. The village was called Francorchamps and the new establishment was named the Hotel des Bruyères, which literally translates as the Hotel of the Heather. The land around Francorchamps was either marshy heathland or thick forest. It was the last village before the German border, which was at the top of the hill after the road to Malmedy rose up after crossing the Eau Rouge stream.

World War I and the Treaty of Versailles which followed altered the borders once again and gave the East Cantons to Belgium, in reparation for some of the damage the Germans had done. The new frontier meant that Francorchamps was no longer the last village before the border and had free access to Malmedy, which had become Belgian. The town was also linked to Stavelot by another road which passed through the hamlet of Masta. So there was a triangle of road in Belgian territory – which almost no-one used. This fact was noticed by Jules de Thiers, the managing director of the La Meuse newspaper, and he proposed using it as a racing circuit, taking Henri Langlois Van Ophem, the chairman of the sporting commission of the Royal Automobile Club Belgium, to lunch at the Hotel des Bruyères to discuss the idea.

The club was looking for a racing circuit that would be fast, cause minimal disruption and be easily accessible for spectators by railway. The concluded that the Francorchamps-Malmedy-Stavelot triangle would be perfect, as it was fast, had a station in each town and the population was sparse. The Mayor of Spa, Baron Joseph de Crawhez, liked the idea. He was an automobilist and with his brother Baron Pierre had had some interesting adventures with automobiles in the early years, driving Panhards into the Sahara Desert, to see if they could get through to Sub-Saharan Africa.

Thus it was all agreed and the first race was planned for a few weeks after the Automobile Club de France revived its Grand Prix at Le Mans, in the summer of 1921. The problem was that the Belgians received only one entry for their race. De Thiers was unperturbed and held the race for motorcycles instead. The riders were excited about the circuit – and the word got out to the car racing people...

And that is why the original Eau Rouge corner was known as the Virage de Ancienne Douane – the Old Custom House Bend.

The Russians are coming...

Given all the recent kerfuffling about Russian influence in the United States, perhaps it is an apt moment to mention that the first Formula 1 United States Grand Prix was organised by a man who was born in Russia... Alexander Edward Ulmann, known as Alec.

There had been some Grand Prix races in the US in the early years of the sport, notably the American Grand Prize on a road course near Savannah, Georgia, in 1908, but Ulmann was the first promoter to bring the F1 World Championship to US shores.

Born in St Petersburg in 1903, Ulmann was the son of a wealthy industrialist, while his mother was a member of the aristocratic Volgensky family. When Alexander was five he became enthralled with automobiles when he saw cars taking part in the St Petersburg-Moscow road race.

In 1917, when he was 13, Russia erupted into revolution and the Ulmann family fled the Bolsheviks and settled in Switzerland, where Alexander was sent to school. He was soon fluent in Russian, French, German and English. He was still fascinated by machines and in 1921 won a place at the Massachusetts Institute of Technology, in Cambridge, Massachusetts (read Boston), where he earned a Master's degree in aeronautical engineering.

He became a naturalised American citizen in the same era – and developed a taste for high-powered American cars. Graduating in 1928, he went to work for Goodyear, his language skills getting him transferred back to Europe, where he soon gained a pilot's licence and flew from country to country in a Kinner-engined Brunner-Winkle Bird biplane, which had been designed for barnstormers. He would become the European agent for the firm.

While in England he met Mary Foote, who was a rather glamorous assistant to Lieutenant Commander Harold Perrin, the director of the Royal Aero Club In London. This organisation issued all UK flying licences. Foote was a well-spoken young beauty, who lived in Weybridge, had attended finishing schools in Switzerland, France and Germany and spoke three languages. They married soon afterwards and Ulmann whisked her away to New York, where he quickly became a leading light in the Automobile Racing Club of America, which later became the SCCA, and she became a celebrated member of the New York social scene.

When the war came, Ulmann was named president of the Dowty Equipment Corporation, a U.S subsidiary of the listed British engineering company which manufactured landing gear and hydraulic systems for aircraft. The company produced more than a million hydraulic units and tens of thousands of undercarriage structures for a range of aircraft. Ulmann realised that after the war there would be huge opportunities in aviation and so he established AE Ulmann Associates Ltd, in order to acquire surplus military aircraft to convert or upgrade them for civilian use. He became the purchasing agent for Lufthansa and Alitalia in the U.S and represented American aviation firms in Europe. The parts business he developed was akin to printing money and it grew rapidly. In 1960 it was merged with Allied International, which did similar work in Asia, creating a global business with Ulmann as its president and key shareholder.

Motor racing remained his passion and hobby. He wrote books about automotive history and his articles appeared in various magazine. He collected Bugattis and Hispano Suizas. He served as chief steward for early road racing events at Watkins Glen, Bridgehampton, Floyd Bennett Field and Westhampton and went to Le Mans in 1950, managing the Briggs Cunningham racing team. He decided on that visit that America ought to have its own international endurance race.

One of his parts warehouses, and his workshops, were located at a Florida airfield called Hendricks Field, which had previously been the main training base for B-17 bomber crews during the wartime years. This had been turned over to the local authorities in Sebring to be used as a civilian airport. Ulmann concluded that Hendricks Field had endless possibilities as a racing circuit, thanks to its intersecting runways and taxiways. He talked the local government into agreeing to the idea and at the end of December 1950 he organised a six hour race, which was won by Fred Wacker and Frank Burrell in a Cadillac-powered Allard. In the course of the event, Ulmann took Florida Governor Fuller Warren for a lap around the track – while the race was in progress.

His European connections enabled him to lobby the necessary authorities and in 1952 the Sebring 12 Hours was launched, as a full scale FIA-sanctioned event and a round of the World Sports Car Championship. This would be held each year with a string of associated social events, which attracted not only Europe's top racers, but also wealthy Americans, who liked to winter in Florida. It wasn't quite Monaco, but there were good parties…

The Ulmanns lived a jet-set life, with an apartment on Park Avenue in New York, a home in the Hamptons and regular trips to big European races, notably Monaco and Le Mans, but also the Targa Florio in Sicily.

The success is the Sebring 12 Hours – which took a few years and some hefty losses – led Ulmann to decide that America was ready for F1 and he did a five-year deal for Sebring to host the United States Grand Prix in 1959, the first F1 race in the U.S.

Fortunately Senator Joe McCarthy was dead by then and so there were never any paranoid claims of Ulmann being involved Communist subversion.

The first race, won by Bruce McLaren, attracted only a small crowd and was a financial disaster. Ulmann decided to move the race to Riverside in California in 1960, but this fared little better and so in 1961 he took up the offer to run the race at Watkins Glen in upstate New York...

An idea in Sweden

There must have been something strange in the air in Jönköping county in southern Sweden in the mid-1960s. The first strange thing was in 1966 when Bengt Erlandson, known to all as "Big Bengt", decided to build a cowboy town in the middle of a Swedish forest, near the village of Kulltorp. Erlandson came up with the idea after being offered 200,000 telegraph poles by the national telephone company. The town was christened High Chaparral. Next door he built a museum of industrial artefacts.

At the same as this was happening, a few mile to the west in the village of Anderstorp a man called Sven Åsberg, known to all as "Smokey", announced to his friends Åke Bengtsson and Bertil Sanell, over coffee one morning, that they were going to build a racing circuit in the wooded marshlands of Stötabomossen, to the south of the town. Åsberg had a successful plastics business but he did not have the kind of money needed to invest in a circuit. His plan was to integrate an airstrip into the facility and to get the local industrialists to fund the idea, on the basis that they would then have an airport which would make the region more accessible to the world. It was 80 miles from Göteborg and 250 miles from Stockholm.

Weirdly, it worked. The charismatic Åsberg sold shares in the project and the circuit was designed by an engineer called Holger Eriksson, with advice from F1 driver Jo Bonnier. The circuit was dominated by its long back straight – the airfield runway – but the rest of the track was twisty with a number of constant radius slightly-banked corners. This made it very difficult to set up cars because one had to find a compromise between the two sections. Oddly, the pits were also separated from the start-finish line, as this was not long enough to meet the necessary requirements. The track hosted its inaugural race on June 16, 1968, and Åsberg shocked everyone by declaring that in five years the circuit would get a Grand Prix. That seemed unlikely at the time. There was little infrastructure to support a big race, with few hotels, although the racing visitors would stay at the High Chaparral and race on dirt roads through the forests to Anderstorp. However, Åsberg was no doubt aware that a new generation of young Swedes were climbing up the racing ladder, notably Ronnie Peterson and Reine Wisell, and he hoped that one or more of them would replace Bonnier in F1. Peterson and Wisell duly made their F1 debuts in 1970 and Peterson was soon established as a star.

Amazingly, on June 17, 1973, (five years and a day after Åsberg's ambitious claim, the first Swedish F1 Grand Prix took place at Anderstorp. There would be five further Swedish GPs, but the deaths of Peterson and Gunnar Nilsson in 1978 meant that it became impossible to keep the event going.

Formula 1 in Cornwall

People have the strangest ideas. In the 1950s some bright spark decided that the English county of Cornwall should host its own Formula 1 races.

For those who don't know, Cornwall is the western part of the south-western peninsular of England. The Cornish people were once racially rather different to the English, with Celtic roots, and a few of their descendants believe Cornwall should have its own assembly, although today it is has one of the older populations compared to other counties in Britain, due to its pleasant climate and attractive countryside which attracts retirees, and because of the outflow of youngsters, moving to find more lively places.

The Cornish F1 races took place on the Davidstow circuit, which was laid out on the runways and taxiways of the disused RAF Davidstow Moor, a Coastal Command airfield that had opened in 1942. The first race meetings were organised in 1952 by the Cornish Vintage Car Club and by the Plymouth Motor Club. The biggest problem at Davidstow was poor weather, with frequent rain and fog. Despite this the first races attracted 3,000 people. The race meetings were planned for Bank Holidays in the hope of drawing bigger crowds.

This seemed to work because in June 1954 there were 20,000 spectators to see the first F1 race, over 20 laps. There were only seven starters and only one real F1 car, the majority of the field being in F2 machinery. The race was won by John Riseley-Pritchard in a Connaught. The meeting had to be abandoned because Horace Gould, who was racing a Kieft, somehow managed to drive his transporter, a converted London bus, into a footbridge, causing it to collapse on to the circuit. There was a second F1 race a couple of months later, in August, but the weather was dreadful again with drizzle and fog. The field was six cars and the race was won by John Coombs in a Lotus.

The final Cornish F1 race was in May 1955. There were six cars: three Connaughts and three Coopers, with victory going to Leslie Marr in a streamlined Connaught.

That was the end of it. F1 cars have not raced in Cornwall since.

Interlaken, Brazil

The first proper motor races in Brazil took place in 1934 on the Gavea road circuit near Rio de Janeiro and two years later the first international drivers began to arrive. The city of São Paulo, naturally, wanted not to be left behind and so hosted a "Grande Premio Cidade de São Paulo." This was not a great success as there was a large accident when a straw bale fell into the path of one of the competitors and the car crashed into the crowd, killing three and injuring 33 others. The races in Rio continued but São Paulo had a different idea.

Back in the 1920s, a British citizen with the usual name of Luiz Romero Sanson, had dreamed up the idea of a satellite city for São Paulo, in keeping with the idea of garden cities which were developed in England in the same era. Born in Trinidad in the Caribbean, and educated in Venezuela, Sanson had settled in Brazil and had made a fortune with Autoestradas SA, a company that built motorways.

To the south of São Paulo, two large reservoirs had been built to provide the city with hydroelectric power. To do this a new road had to be built and Autoestradas SA was brought in to do the work. Sanson had previously acquired more land than he needed when he built the Congonhas Airport and he decided to do the same between the two lakes and then hired a French architect called Alfred Agache to design a garden city.

The lakes reminded Agache of Interlaken in Switzerland and so it was decided to call the area Interlagos, which means "between lakes". However the Wall Street Crash in 1929 meant that the financial situation changed and soon afterwards Brazil underwent a revolution and so nothing much was done although Sanson continued to plan, including a large recreational area in the project, which would include a beach, created with sand trucked up from the sea at Santos, and a motor racing circuit.

He wanted to build a great track and studied other circuits around the world and concluded that the best design would be one based on Roosevelt Raceway, near New York, which curled around on itself. Construction finally began in 1938 and the track was paved the following year but there was no money for any other facilities and it would be many years before grandstands and pit facilities were constructed. The circuit was to have been inaugurated in November 1939 but the weather was bad and so the opening was delayed until May 1940, when 15,000 people watched the first race.

Interlagos was sold to the city of São Paulo for a nominal sum in 1954.

A man for all continents

The Brazilian architect Lolô Cornelsen was a fairly prolific designer of racing circuits in his day. He penned Rio de Janeiro's Jacarepaguá, (1966), plus the tracks at Curitiba (1967), Estoril (1972) and a little-known circuit in Luanda in Angola, which opened three weeks before Estoril.

The Portuguese colony on the west coast of Africa had seen its first motor races in the late 1950s. These were primarily sports car races on a street circuit in Luanda, but they attracted international entries and the ambition existed in Angola to host F1 races. With this in mind, Cornelsen was commissioned to design an Autódromo Internacional de Luanda out in the country to the south west of the city, close to the Atlantic coast.

Less than a year after the new circuit opened, there was a military coup in Portugal and the new government planned to make Angola independent, in order to stop a long-running armed struggle that dated back to 1961. Around half a million Portuguese departed as a result of the plan, the majority of them being the country's only skilled workers. The result was a power vacuum and then a full blown civil war, as different armed factions fought for control of Angola. This war would go on until 2002, by which time the Autódromo was out of date. It is still there today, but the city has now grown around it...

An African heart

Count Ferdinand de Lesseps was a man of much vigour. A diplomat of distinction, who served France in many different countries, he had a rather tragic private life, losing three of his five children when they were young, the third in 1853 just a few days after the death of his wife, at the age of only 33. He decided to change his life dramatically and retired from public service and began to promote the idea of a 75-mile canal through the isthmus of Suez, in order to link the Mediterranean Sea and the Red Sea. It took 15 years to raise the money and complete the project, but on November 17 1869 the Suez Canal opened. It is rare that men achieve things that truly change the world, but the Suez Canal certainly did.

Eight days after the canal was opened the 64-year-old Count de Lesseps married 21-year-old Louise-Hélène Autard de Bragard – and they proceeded to have no fewer than 12 children, in the years that followed. The youngest, Gisèle, was born in 1885, when de Lesseps was a mere 79 years of age, at which point he was in the process of building the Panama Canal. Alas, it all went badly. The company failed and the Count was convicted of bribing French politicians to fund the project. He avoided prison, but died in disgrace in 1894.

His children were an adventurous bunch: three of his sons were killed in World War I (two of them having been Olympic fencers), a fourth son was the second man to fly the English Channel and was later presumed lost while conducting an aerial survey of the coast of Canada.

One of his daughters married a Spanish duke while Gisèle, the baby of the family, was 21 when she was swept off her feet in 1906 by a dashing cavalryman called Louis Lacaze. His family owned the very grand Chateau de Saint-Pierre-du-Perray, and both came from dazzling families with long histories of soldiers, politicians, businessmen, writers and diplomats. His mother had died soon after he was born, but even Louis's stepmother came from a very rich family.

Louis and Gisèle would produce five children, the youngest being Robert, who was born in 1917. He had obviously inherited some of the family's adventurous genes because when he was 19 he travelled to the Atlas Mountains, 50 miles from Marrakesh and built the first ski refuge at Oukaïmeden, at 10,500 ft above sea level. He would return to France after that but he soon tried motor racing at Montlhéry – and he liked it. During the war he was sent to Morocco where he completed his studies under the Vichy government but in 1942 Morocco was liberated and Lacaze spent his time after that as a sports instructor. He was a successful skier, a good footballer and he would end up running the Service de la Jeunesse et des Sports for the city.

In 1948, keen to develop Oukaimeden, he set up a transport business to provide access and supplies to the ski area. He did this in league with Baron Maurice de Castex, a former fighter pilot. The two would also become partners in a garage on the Avenue Landais, one of the wide boulevards, built in the Gueliz district of the city during the period when Morocco was a French protectorate. It would become a Simca dealership. In 1949 Lacaze married a gym teacher Janine Armand.

He began in Moroccan motor sport with rudimentary street races around Marrakesh after which he became a star of Moroccan rallying, taking part in the

1951 Rally of Morocco in a Renault 4CV and finishing sixth, although he would win the event in 1954 in a Simca Aronde and again in 1967 with a Renault 8 Gordini. He raced in many other local rallies and in various touring car "Grands Prix" in Tangiers, Agadir, Marrakech and Casablanca. In March 1956 the French protectorate was ended and many of the French settlers decided to depart, worried what the future would hold. Decaze remained and raced afterwards with a Moroccan licence.

The following year Sultan Mohammed declared himself King and to show the world about Morocco, he agreed to fund the construction of a new racing circuit, using the public roads in the Ain-Diab district of Casablanca. Part of this track ran along the coast road and the return leg was inland in the desert. It was fast and in October 1957 it hosted the Grand Prix de Maroc, a non-championship F1 race, won by Jean Behra in a Maserati.

There were no local drivers involved. The King pushed for a World Championship race in 1958 and the FIA agreed that the Moroccan Grand Prix would be the World Championship showdown. That year Lacaze went to France and competed in several events including the Le Mans 24 Hours meeting with a works Gordini, which he shared with "Charles Rinen" although the car retired in the race before he could drive it. He also finished fourth in the Tour de France automobile race in a Porsche 356 Carrera. As a result he was allowed to take part in the Grand Prix.

It was going to be the first African World Championship F1 event and the King wanted "an African" driver and so journalist Jabby Crombac organised a deal for Lacaze (entered with his Moroccan licence) and André Guelfi (a local settler) to race a pair of Formula 2 Cooper-Climax T45s, which were being run by Ken Tyrrell. The race was the championship showdown between Stirling Moss and Mike Hawthorn and while Moss won the race, Hawthorn took the title – and became Britain's first World Champion. The same day Stuart Lewis-Evans suffered terrible burns when his engine exploded at high speed. Although he was flown home to Britain, he died a week later.

Out of the international spotlight, Lacaze did a very decent job and finished 14th, five laps behind the winner, but only a lap down on the best F2 runner, Jack Brabham, in a similar car. Lacaze was on the same lap as Brabham's team-mate Bruce McLaren…

F1 would not return to Morocco again, largely because of the accident, but Lacaze went back to Le Mans in 1959 and 1960 in Porsches which he shared with Jean Kerguen. He retired on both occasions with mechanical troubles. He went on competing in the 1960s and then his son Marc started competing. Robert did eventually move to France where he lived in Cannes until his 99th year. When he died in 2015 he was the oldest surviving F1 driver.

His wish was to be buried in the European cemetery in Marrakesh.

The boy from Bulawayo

Jody Scheckter is the only African driver to have won the Formula 1 World Championship, and indeed the only one to have won Grands Prix, the first being in Sweden in 1974. That came seven years after another African came tantalizingly close to a sensational victory...

It is a story which began in the city of Bulawayo, in the British Crown colony of Southern Rhodesia. This was a gold mining town on the Matzheumhlope River, surrounded by rich grazing country. It was the richest city in the colony.

It was also the birthplace of John Maxwell Love. He grew up there, attended the Bulawayo Technical High School, and was employed as an apprentice electrical fitter until World War II, when he became one of the early recruits of the Southern Rhodesian Reconnaissance Regiment. This tiny unit was soon scooped up into the South African 6th Armoured Division which was sent to Egypt in the middle of 1943. It was then fitted out with Sherman tanks and in April 1944 arrived in Italy to take part in the campaign to clear the Germans out. Towards the end of the war, Love was stationed near Monza and took a spin around the old Autodromo, riding a captured Zundapp motorcycle. Love loved it and he soon became a dispatch rider during the final campaigns of the war.

When it was over, he went back to Bulawayo, at the age of 21 and started racing motorcycles. He did not switch to cars until he was nearly 30. In 1954 he bought a Cooper-JAP Formula 3 car and became a regular competitor on the dirt tracks of Southern Rhodesia. After some success and many thrills and spills, he decided to race in South Africa in 1957 and a year after that went to England where he raced for Ken Tyrrell in Formula Junior all over Europe and won the British Touring Car Championship in a Mini Cooper.

He seemed on the verge of an F1 career, but in 1962 had a big crash in Albi and crushed his arm. He had several operations but it seemed like his career was over. He went back home but decided to try local surgeons. After two operations, he was soon back in action. He got a break in 1964 when John Cooper telephoned and asked him to fly to Italy to stand in for the injured Phil Hill at Monza. There were mechanical troubles and no spares and so Love did not qualify. He went home again and concentrated his efforts on winning the next six consecutive South African Championships. He continued to compete in international events and in 1966 acquired the Cooper-Climax T79 Tasman car that Bruce McLaren had raced. The following year he decided to enter the car in the South African GP. This required extra fuel tanks, but the car was light thanks to its smaller engine than the average F1 unit.

The 1967 South African GP was scheduled for Monday, January 2, at Kyalami and most of the F1 teams showed up with 1966 cars. Ferrari and McLaren didn't go at all, but it was still a good field and Love stunned them all by qualifying fifth on the grid, ahead of John Surtees, Graham Hill, Jochen Rindt and Jackie Stewart!

Come race day, he made a bad start and dropped to 10th, but others hit trouble and he gradually moved up the order. Denny Hulme led but gradually Love rose to second, ahead of Pedro Rodriguez. On lap 61 of 80 Hulme drove into the pits with brake trouble. Love was leading, with 19 laps to go. For the next 12 laps, the local fans celebrated an astonishing achievement, but with seven laps to go the car started misfiring. The pump to the auxiliary tanks had packed up and Love realised he would have to stop. By the time he rejoined, Rodriguez was 20 seconds ahead and there was no time to catch him. But even second place was an amazing achievement…

Love was then 43 but he continued winning the local championship with backing coming from the Gunston Cigarette Company of Rhodesia, as the country had become in 1965. This was the very first tobacco sponsorship of motor racing. In the end he retired to Bulawayo and stayed there, despite all the problems the country faced in the 1970, until independence and peace came in 1979. But with that came Robert Mugabe. Love ran his garage in Bulawayo until he died at the age of 80 in 2005.

A guest at Kyalami

Wilhelm Rampf – known as Willy – is not a big F1 name like Adrian Newey or Ross Brawn, but he's remarkable in that he has been successful in three completely different motorsport disciplines: Formula 1, the World Rally Championship and with motorcycles on the Paris-Dakar.

Rampf was always mad about motorcycles and took part in a few enduro events in his spare time while he was an apprentice aviation electrician and then an engineering student. In 1978 he worked as a mechanic on the very first Paris-Dakar. BMW was not officially involved, but Frenchman Jean-Claude Morellet, who raced as "Fenouil", rode a prototype BMW 800cc motorcycle and was running second until an engine failure on the penultimate stage.

BMW saw the potential of the Dakar and Rampf joined the company and worked on the development of bikes that would win the Dakar with Hubert Auriol in 1981 and 1983 and Gaston Rahier in 1984 and 1985. When the project ended he moved on to work as a test engineer for BMW South Africa, based in Pretoria.

When F1 visited Kyalami in 1993 Rampf was a Sauber guest, having been invited by former BMW colleague Leo Ress, the Swiss team's technical director. Fascinated by the F1 technology, Willy expressed an interest in joining the team and six months later was thrown in at the deep end, as race engineer for Heinz-Harald Frentzen. Things went well, but when Frentzen moved to Williams, Rampf was less interested in the drivers who followed and decided to go back to BMW, which was planning a new Paris-Dakar programme. He was put in charge. This would result in two consecutive Dakar victories for rider Richard Sainct before Rampf was lured back to Sauber as Technical Director in 2000.

He would remain in the role for the next 10 years, including under BMW ownership between 2005 and 2009. During that time, the team won its first (and only) victory, thanks to Robert Kubica in Canada in 2008, but then BMW pulled the plug and Sauber struggled and Rampf decided it was time to move on and handed over his role to James Key in 2010. A year later Willy was appointed technical director of Volkswagen Motorsport, overseeing the design of the Polo R WRC, which has since won four WRC Drivers' and four Manufacturers' titles between 2013 and 2016…

Unusual backgrounds

Air and water are both fluids and they behave in similar fashions as they flow around obstacles. The design of F1 cars, as we know, depends on efficient aerodynamics and we tend to think of designers in this field coming from the world of aerospace. But, those who study the flow of water can be just as useful. The current Technology Director of the all-powerful Mercedes AMG Petronas team, Geoff Willis, is a case in point. His F1 career began 26 years ago when he began to do some consulting work with Leyton House Racing, which was then under the technical leadership of a young Adrian Newey. The team had a consultant who also consulted with Britain's America's Cup consortium at the time, known as Blue Arrow. This had built a startlingly different kind of yacht to all the other challengers, known as "Radical", for obvious reasons. The hydrodynamicist on Radical was Willis.

An engineering graduate from Cambridge, Willis had worked initially for the scientific research association known as British Maritime Technology, which had previously been a government institution. Based in Teddington, it studied all manner of different things, many of them secret, such as the design of submarines and torpedoes. While he was doing his research work, Willis also gained a PhD in Engineering Science from Exeter University, specializing in hydrodynamics. A while later he was approached by Blue Arrow and asked to join the design team. Unfortunately, Radical was rather too radical and in October 1988, while doing test runs off the coast of Falmouth, the vessel hit a large wave, while travelling at high speed. The bow dug into the water and the yacht pitchpoled, fracturing the hull. The boat was not rebuilt.

The design process had, however, introduced Willis to the new science of computational fluid dynamics, using computer models to simulate fluid flows and thus it was that he became a valuable person to Mr Newey. It was a short-lived relationship because after just a few months Newey was fired by Leyton House (just before the cars came good) and he landed at Williams. He called in Willis and so Geoff joined the team full-time and when Adrian left for McLaren in 1997, Willis became Chief Aerodynamicist of Williams and from there went on to become Technical Director of BAR and Red Bull Racing before landing at Mercedes in 2011.

Being a big bloke

The designer of the first Jordan F1 car was Ulsterman Gary Anderson. He went on to become technical director at Stewart Grand Prix and Jaguar before beginning a career in broadcasting. Gary is a big bloke. Like Raymond Chandler's Moose Malloy, he's "not more than six feet five inches tall and not wider than a beer truck" and it was his size and strength which landed him his first job in F1 on the basis that he could lift a Cosworth DFV engine on his own.

From Coleraine, Anderson was fascinated by motor racing in his teens and was involved in some less-than-legal road races before he decided to leave troubled Northern Ireland to become a racing driver in England. It didn't work out as planned and so Gary found work as a mechanic with Motor Racing Stables at Brands Hatch, before moving to Brabham to build Formula 3 cars. As a result his heavy-lifting skills were noticed and he became an F1 mechanic.

He learned about F1 design by working with Gordon Murray before moving on to McLaren and then set up his own racing car company, called Anson. He ran a competitive European Formula 3 team, his bitter rival being one Eddie Jordan. Anderson moved in to engineer Roberto Moreno to the F3000 title and was then asked to design the Reynard Formula 3000 cars before being talked into joining Jordan by his loquacious ex-enemy. He designed the Jordan 191, one of the most beautiful F1 cars ever built.

Anderson was awarded an honorary doctorate by the University of Ulster in 2014 and today in involved with a company called Typhoon, manufacturing electric motor-assisted composite bicycles.

An F1 car in a ditch

Gary Anderson was driving home from work one day, early in 1989, when he was surprised to see what looked like a racing monocoque in a ditch beside the road. It is not what you expect to see in Warwickshire and so Anderson stopped his car and went to inspect.

He was astonished to discover that it was, indeed, a monocoque and it looked like an F1 car. He noted that the chassis had been badly smashed and recognised that the damage had probably been the result of a failed crash-test at the nearby MIRA facility in Nuneaton. His conclusion was that the chassis had probably been dumped by a disappointed team, on its way home.

A little research revealed that it was exactly that. The First-Judd L189 had been entered in the Formula 1 World Championship that year. In order to compete it needed to undergo crash testing and, as Anderson had concluded, it had failed these tests in comprehesive fashion.

It was a story that dated back to the summer of 1988 when former racer Lamberto Leoni, the owner of the First Racing Formula 3000 team, which had been established in 1987, decided that he wanted to become a Formula 1 team owner in 1989. The rules were changing. A lot of other people had the same idea and there were an impressive 40 entries accepted by the FIA in December that year.

Leoni asked his chief engineer in Formula 3000, Brazilian Richard Divila, who had worked in F1 with the Fittipaldi brothers, to design a Grand Prix car for him. Divila did the first layout and the pre-design work, but then went back to work on the March 88B Formula 3000 car which was causing the team difficulties at the time. The result was a victory for Pierluigi Martini a few weeks later at Enna with podiums at Brands Hatch and Birmingham.

The F1 design was left in the hands of Gianni Marelli, who had worked at Ferrari in the late 1960s before moving to Autodelta in 1971, where he worked on the Alfa Romeo F1 cars before departing to do consulting work from 1981 onwards. The First Racing tub was built by a carbon composite company near Turin. When Divila saw the result of the work he demanded that his name be removed from all First Racing literature. He considered the resulting chassis to be unsafe and advised drivers not to go anywhere near it. He later remarked that the chassis was good for nothing except perhaps for use as "an interesting flowerpot", believing that the monocoque had not been properly cured in the production process and so would delaminate in an accident. He left the team and accepted an offer to design F1 cars for Ligier. When the Italian magazine Autosprint linked his name to the project he visited First Racing with two lawyers in tow and initiated legal action against the team.

While all of this was going on, the car was completed and in the early part of December 1988 it was shaken down at Misano by Gabriele Tarquini. It then appeared in the Formula One Indoor Trophy at the Bologna Motorshow, with Tarquini driving. Then it needed to be crash-tested...

Although the chassis was destroyed in the test, as Divila had predicted, the design still existed – even if it was too late to build anything new for the 1989 season. The team withdrew its entry and the sponsorship package collapsed.

In the summer of 1989 Leoni sold the design to an Italian entrepreneur named Ernesto Vita who had plans to enter F1 with a team called Life Racing Engines, with an interesting W12 engine designed by former Ferrari engineer Franco Rocchi. The car was built by Marelli, but the resulting project was disastrous, as the engine barely ever ran without a problem. The team eventually fell part because the money dried up.

A dream which did not come true

Most people get one chance to make it in Formula 1 - and it doesn't always work out well.

Before the war Gianpaulo Volpini tuned Lancia Aprilia sports cars in his garage in Milan and when the war was over he went back into the same business, but this time building his own chassis with 1100cc engines and bodywork by the Milanese coachbuilder Carrozzeria Colli. This proved to be quite successful and Volpini then diversified into the 500cc Formula 3 in 1951, his Gilera motorcycle engine-powered cars enjoying some success, despite the fierce competition in the formula. In 1953 Frenchman Georges Chazelet even managed to win a race in Marseilles in a Volpini.

It was at this point that the 26-year-old Mario Alborghetti arrived on the scene.

He was the son of a wealthy textile manufacturer who started racing in 1950 in a Fiat Topolino before moving on to win the Argegno-Lanzo d'Intelvi hillclimb, near Como, in 1951 with a Lancia Aprilia. He took part in the Stella Alpina Rally and the Mille Miglia in a Lancia Aurelia and drove a similar car for Lancia Corse in 1953 in the Susa-Moncenisio hillclimb, finishing third in class. He also competed in the Coppa Sant'Ambroeus at Monza and in the Giro di Sicilia and Coppa della Toscana road races. His experience was entirely in sports cars, but he dreamed of becoming a F1 driver and asked Volpini to build him a car.

Like many engineers, Volpini was a practical man and concluded that there was more chance of success if one bought a decent racing car and modified it, rather than trying to reinvent the wheel. Thus he used Alborghetti's money to acquire one of the Scuderia Milano Maserati 4CLTs, which had raced F1 in 1950.

These had been powered by a pre-war supercharged 1.5-litre engine, designed in 1939 by Ernesto Maserati. After the war the cars had been acquired by Scuderia Milano and the engines were modified by Mario Speluzzi, a Professor of Engineering at the Politecnico di Milano, who had developed the engine for use in powerboats. He added two-stage supercharging and the engine was renamed Speluzzi. It first appeared at the French GP in 1950 in the hands of Felice Bonetto. It was clear straight away that this would not be able to compete with the latest machinery at the time and the project faded away.

However with a new engine formula in 1954, Volpini reckoned that with a reworked chassis and a stretched Maserati engine, the result might be competitive and called in engine-builder Egidio Arzani to transform the 1.5-litre engine into a 2.5-litre. Attractive new bodywork was created by Carrozzeria Colli.

Scuderia Volpini was ready to go into action by April 1955 and headed off to Pau, in the south-west of France for a non-championship F1 race. The Arzani-Volpini 001 was well-presented and well-engineered but it was not very fast and Alborghetti qualified 19 secs slower than pole.

The race, held of the Easter Monday bank holiday, attracted a big crowd and while they cheered for Jean Behra's Maserati 250F against the Lancias, no-one paid much attention to Alborghetti, who made three early pit stops. At the start of his 20th lap, he came down to the tight right-hand hairpin near the Station, the first corner, and Jacques Pollet went down the inside to lap Alborghetti. For reasons unknown, the Arzani-Volpini went straight on, apparently without any attempt being made to slow the car. It ran into hay bales with considerable force, the driver's helmet flew off in the impact and the driver died almost instantly as the result of fractures to the vertebrae in his neck. A number of spectators were injured in the crash, although the car itself was not badly damaged. The team was not seen again until the Italian GP at Monza in September, where Luigi Piotti was due to drive, but things went wrong and he did not take part in qualifying.

Volpini turned his attention to building a record car in 1956 and then when Formula Junior began in 1958 he bought more racing cars, continuing production until 1963.

How to start an industry

The first man to die at the wheel of a Formula 1 car was a little-known 29-year-old Anglo-American called Cameron Earl. He was an engineer and the team manager of Bob Gerard Racing. Earl had taken a pre-war ERA, updated to F1 spec, to the old Lindley aerodrome, better known today as the home of the Motor Industry Research Association (MIRA), for a test run one evening in June 1952. The car flipped at high speed and Earl was crushed. He survived until the following morning.

Earl is, however, rather more than a sad footnote in motor racing history and is seen by many as one of the key figures in the history of the British motorsport industry, thanks to a 141-page technical analysis he wrote of the 1930s German Grand Prix teams. This included a huge amount of detail, revealing the secrets of the Mercedes and Auto Union Grand Prix cars.

How did an unknown 25-year-old Army officer get to be the author of such an important document?

Well, like many great stories, it began in Scarborough. This is a Yorkshire seaside resort where an American soldier decided to settle with a Yorkshire girl after World War I. They had a child and when the young Cameron was 17, World War II broke out. He was called up and assigned to the Royal Armoured Corps. His technical abilities were soon spotted, however, and he so he was posted to the Department of Tank Design in Chobham, Surrey, where he joined the School of Tank Technology. This analysed foreign machinery (allied and enemy) and wrote reports about the innovations, so that they could be used in future British tank designs. Earl was later sent on attachment to the Admiralty Research Laboratory in Teddington, where he met a young engineer called John Cooper, who was working on the secret design of a one-man submarine.

After the Normandy landings in 1944, Allied intelligence began to produce reports on the German military and industrial information that emerged. These were written by teams of scientists, working for the Combined Intelligence Objectives

Sub-Committee (CIOS). Once Germany was defeated, the British created their own British Intelligence Objectives Sub-Committee (BIOS) and continued the same work, creating 2,000 reports on German technology. Earl co-authored a report on German infra-red technology and this led to him being given a hurried commission as a Second Lieutenant in July 1945 in order to give him officer status so that he could acquire more information from captured Germans.

He was keen on motorsport and proposed that BIOS look into Germany's automobile industry – and the pre-war Grand Prix teams. He went to Germany for a month in April 1947, obtained access to all the required files and blueprints and even interviewed old engineers. He submitted his report in March 1948 and it was published by His Majesty's Stationery Office six months later. It was entitled "An Investigation into the Development of German Grand Prix Cars 1934-1939".

By the time the report came out, he had left the Army and was studying mechanical engineering. He would then set up his own consulting business – Earl Automotive Patents Ltd. He found time to take part in the 1950 Monte Carlo Rally, with a Standard Vanguard. The consulting business was slow and do he went to work with Gerard, developing a hydrostatic infinitely-variable transmission for the ERA.

Information is power, so they say, and Earl's insights played an important role in shaping the thinking of a whole generation of young engineers who flooded into the sport after the war, looking for excitement. These included his pal John Cooper, who would lead the revolution that created Britain's motorsport industry of today with his rear-engined cars.

A concept that the Germans had looked at in depth…

A bit of a dodgy geezer

Espionage has been part of motorsport since the sport began, with teams and manufacturers stealing one another's secrets. It was, of course, a sport in which many car dealers were involved, and that profession has always had a rather poor reputation for its dodgy dealings.

Joseph Michael Kelly, known as Joe, did little to change that image – but he was certainly a colourful character…

As the name suggests, Kelly was born in Ireland in 1913, before the country won its independence from Britain. He left school at 13 and learned a few tricks working in the street markets of Dublin, before training as a railway fitter and then becoming a tram driver. He moved on to drive buses, although he ran into trouble in the late 1930s, when he crashed while racing a fellow bus driver through the streets of Dublin. He departed, rather hurriedly, so they say, to England and settled in London, doing a bit of this and a bit of that. He worked with road haulage firms, got married and started a family. With Ireland being neutral, he was not in the forces. Looking to make more money, he joined the car trade.

There was a lot of money to be made from cars at the end of the war. Purchase tax was payable on all new cars, with double purchase tax on cars that cost more than £1,000. The goal of this policy was to encourage the UK manufacturers to favour exports. Domestic buyers had to sign covenants with the British Motor Trade Association committing them to not sell their cars for 12 months or longer. This meant that demand far exceeded supply and big profits could be made on covenant-free cars, particularly high-end sports cars, such as MGs, Rileys and Alvises. In order to dodge the rules, some dealers paid for new cars, but arranged for others to sign the covenants. They then sold the cars at a substantial profit. A young Roy Salvadori fell foul of such behaviour in 1949, in a legal action which stopped such activity. By then, however, a few car dealers had made small fortunes, which paid for them to go racing.

Kelly was friends with Salvadori (and others) and was soon sufficiently wealthy to buy 70 acres of land on the main Dublin to Naas highway. He established a garage called the Red Cow Service Station and still had sufficient money to buy a Maserati 6CM voiturette. He began taking part in major racing events, notably the 1949 BRDC Trophy at the new Silverstone circuit. Keen to move up the ladder he bought an Alta GP3, the first British-built Grand Prix car after the war, and in the summer of 1950 this led to an invitation to race in the British GP – the very first round of the FIA Formula 1 World Championship.

Kelly enjoyed success in Ireland, where the opposition was not as strong, notably at the Curragh, with a Jaguar C-Type. He soon modified the Alta to such an extent that he decided to rename it as the IRA (Irish Racing Automobile). The initials of the car were, of course, the same as those of the terrorist group known as the Irish Republican Army, although in that period the IRA was not as active as it would become later in the decade. The cars appeared in 1952 and 1953.

Early in 1954 Kelly had a new idea. With the help of a local restaurant owner who spoke Italian, he sent a telegram to Enzo Ferrari requesting an audience. When the reply came back, Kelly was so keen to know what it said that he went to his friend's house in the middle of the night and threw a brick through a window to wake up the poor translator. The message welcomed a visit and Kelly and his translator set off to Italy. They met Ferrari and a deal was struck for him to become the Ferrari dealer for Ireland – and to buy a 750 Monza Spyder Scaglietti. It was the first such car to be sold to a privateer, but the relationship did not develop well. The car arrived unassembled, which did not please Kelly, and he was also upset that he had been sold a car with a five-speed racing gearbox, but it arrived with a production four-speed unit.

Ferrari sent the right gearbox after Kelly complained, but was unimpressed when the car raced in a green livery. Kelly beat his own lap record at The Curragh and shared the car with Desmond Titterington in the Tourist Trophy at Dundrod. They then won the Leinster Trophy at Wicklow and the car was then driven by Mike Hawthorn in the Goodwood Trophy.

Titterington was offered a factory Jaguar drive at that point and soon afterwards, despite promising Ferrari he would not reveal the technical details of the car, Kelly handed over the 750 Monza to Jaguar, which stripped it down and analysed how it was superior to the Jaguar D-Types it raced against. The D-Types were then modified and in 1955 Jaguar won Le Mans with Mike Hawthorn and Ivor Bueb, followed in 1956 by Ron Flockhart and Ninian Sanderson and in 1957 by Flockhart and Bueb. Ferrari did not win again until 1958. One might argue that Kelly was responsible for these successes… In any case, he soon sold the Ferrari to Peter Whitehead.

In April 1955 Kelly crashed his Jaguar C-Type heavily at Oulton Park, in a heat for the British Empire Trophy. He went into the commentary box and suffered serious leg injuries. While recovering he met Phyllis Purcell, who would become his second wife. They settled permanently in England after that and Kelly built up a series of car dealerships in the course of the next 14 years, often trading cars and motorcycles with another dealer called Bernie Ecclestone. In 1969 Kelly sold everything and moved back to Ireland where he built up an impressive property portfolio in the 1970s and 1980s – not to mention a car collection. He competed from time to time in races and hillclimbs until he was in his sixties.

Kelly would lose most of his fortune in a property crash in the 1980s and he returned to England to settle in Neston in Cheshire. He was diagnosed with Alzheimer's disease and died late in 1993 at the age of 80.

A murderer in the paddock

Formula 1 is a world of extreme people. They tend to be ambitious, highly competitive, aggressive – and some are pretty dysfunctional. We have seen some really colourful characters over the years, but Rainer Walldorf is probably the most extreme example.

For a start, his name wasn't really Rainer Walldorf, but rather Klaus Walz, or at least we think it was. It was also Peter Walz when it suited him. In fact, there is no real evidence which proves it is the same Klaus Walz who raced in the late 1970s and early 1980s in Interserie, Aurora F1 and even Formula 2. It is often assumed it is the same man, but it doesn't really make sense. Klaus Walz was a wanted man under his own name and so it would have been extremely unwise to turn up in racing with a different name, as he might very easily bump into someone who knew his real name...

In any case, while the records from the racing world have Walz listed as having been born in Ettlingen, near Karlsruhe in 1942, the company filings that link him to F1 have him born in 1944.

His primary accomplice was his nephew, a man who used the unlikely name of Gordon Walz. But then he also used the names Patrick, Peter and Klaus Sorajowski, a name which has its roots in the Balkans, but may also have been "borrowed" from the boss of a haulage firm in Wiesbaden.

Anyway, Walldorf and Sorajowski had a couple of companies using these names: Comstock Development and L'Art Mineral, both of them headquartered in Cannes, although the directors used different combinations of the various names.

Walz presented himself as a dealer in exotic luxury cars, but the authorities would eventually conclude that he was actually the mastermind behind a vast international network dealing with black market stolen super cars. The centre of this network seems to have been a facility in the town of Desio, just up the road from Monza. One supposes that this was an Aladdin's garage where plates were changed and cars resprayed.

For whatever reason, however, it was in that area that in 1989 the two men and a Canadian accomplice murdered an Italian mechanic called Antonio Tonetto. It was a particularly nasty crime as they locked him in the boot of a Fiat Panda and set fire to the car. In the end it seems that they opened the trunk and shot the unfortunate individual to silence his screams. Two others bodies would pop up later in a villa near Lisbon in Portugal and, according to Interpol, Walz also had the blood of a fourth murder (a Swiss) on his hands.

Walz appeared in F1 – as Rainer Walldorf – in August 1992. There was a big fanfare with the purchase of a majority shareholding in the Larrousse F1 team, which had previously been owned by the French sports car company MVS Venturi. The Comstock company had a decidedly dodgy business plan, based on the unlikely-sounding idea of having "investment sponsorship", with the money invested in the team being paid back in full after five years, thus giving sponsors free exposure. It would to be a membership scheme, organized by a London wheeler-dealer.

The Comstock name suggested that Walz believed that the company would make a lot of money, the Comstock Lode having been a huge silverfield discovered in Nevada in 1859, which generated vast fortunes over a 15 year period.

Within a few weeks of the Larrousse announcement, Walz and Sorajewski were arrested when French police raided a villa in Valbonne, a chic commune near Mougins, on the Cote d'Azur. There are various stories about what happened but some say that Walz pulled out a hand grenade and held a police inspector hostage, before handcuffing the other policemen and then disappearing with $500,000 in cash. The duo escaped to Italy, but a month later were tracked down to a hotel in Munich. The police raided and Sorajewski was apprehended, but Walz refused to give up and, after a nine-hour siege, shot himself. The property developer involved in the F1 concept would disappear when his empire fell apart a few years later.

An over-enthusiast

Piero Dusio was a footballer who was good enough to play for Juventus for a few games in 1921 and 1922 before he suffered a knee injury and was forced to look for work elsewhere, going into the textile business. In 1926, when he was 26 years of age, he started his own business called Manifatture Bosco SA, which produced waterproof materials. This led to diversification into the manufacturing of clothing and later sporting goods such as tennis rackets and racing bicycles. In 1932 he signed a contract with Benito Mussolini's government to provide uniforms for the Italian army. His other businesses included finance and real estate and the Juventus football team itself.

The name Cisitalia appeared with the merger of four companies to establish Manifatture Bosco - Compagnia Industriale Sportiva Italiana in 1942. In 1946 this changed its name to Cisitalia and the company raison d'être expanded to include the manufacture of industrial machines and vehicles. His money had paid for a racing career, beginning in 1929 with an entry in the Mille Miglia. He would go on to compete in the race every year until 1938, while also racing single-seaters, is best result being sixth in the Italian GP in 1936. He then set up Scuderia Torino, just before the war broke out. During the war years he commissioned Fiat's Dante Giacosa to design him a 1100cc racing car for the post-war era. The D46 was soon in action after the war finished and Dusio used one to win the Coppa Brezzi in Turin in September 1946.

The car quickly became popular and was used by such stars as Tazio Nuvolari and Louis Chiron. In 1947 Piero Taruffi took one of the cars to win his class in the Italian national championship while Cisitalia expanded to produce some sports cars as well and the cars did well on the Mille Miglia and the Targa Florio. It was at this point that Porsche's Italian distributor Carlo Abarth - who was running a Cisitalia for Scuderia Scagliarini - approached Dusio and asked him if he would like to build a Grand Prix car that had been designed by Ferdinand Porsche. The engine was a 1.5-litre supercharged flat-12, which had been created for, but never raced by Auto Union in 1939.

The car was built in Italy with help of ex-AutoUnion engineer Robert Eberan von Eberhorst. In truth the car was way to complicated for Dusio's operation, as it also included four-wheeled drive, a sequential gear-shift and a rear-mounted transaxle that channelled power to a front differential. It was called the Type 360 and appeared in 1948 but did not race much because Dusio ran out of money. The factory had to be closed down in 1948 and the sports cars were handed over to Abarth. Dusio himself disappeared to Argentina, where he started a new car company called Autocar, although this was without much success. Cisitalia went into liquidation in 1949. Douse paid Porsche a great deal of money and part of this was used to but Ferdinand Porsche his freedom, as he was incarcerated in Dijon on very dubious charges. The money was paid and he was released in August 1947. One prototype was finished but Dusio ran out of money and the car was left undeveloped. Today the car is in the Porsche Museum in Stuttgart.

How not to do it

Like oil, sugar changed the world. The demand for the flavouring led to lands being seized, slaves being traded, vast fortunes being made and all manner of nefarious acts. Cane sugar came first, with relatively small plantations able to produce wealth that could sustain European aristocratic lifestyles. And then in 1747 a German chemist called Andreas Marggraf discovered there was sucrose in beetroot. It was more difficult to extract but experiments in Silesia made it economically viable.

The Napoleonic Wars led to the French banning the importation of sugar, not wanting to provide the British with funding for the wars. So the French turned to Margraff's ideas and an sugar beet industry emerged, fortunes were made and the newly-rich married among themselves creating vast empires. They diversified, bought land, became politicians and won titles.

One of the richest men in France by the end of the 19th Century was sugar baron Gustave Lebaudy. His daughter Geneviève married Charles Bourlon de Rouvre, another sugar magnate. He would become a celebrated parliamentarian. Later their grandson Evrard presided quietly over the family empire, but indulged in his passion for film-making. His son Cyril, born in 1945, was educated in schools across Europe, so that he spoke all the right languages, and then joined the family empire, working in the sugar and then audiovisual companies.

Cyril was passionate about racing cars and took part in some motoring adventures, notably the Abidjan-Nice race in the mid-1970s, driving a Range Rover.

His life changed completely in 1979 when his father was stabbed to death by his valet (Yes, the butler DID do it). Cyril was 33 and inherited the entire family empire, including real estate holdings, the sugar refinery and 28 other companies. He modernized sugar production and added to the conglomerate, buying control of the Fraissinet transport company in 1981, including the Transair airline. In 1987 he launched into the film industry by acquiring Financière Robur, which owned an archive of 650 movies. He also began producing movies and he expanded in real estate as well, buying a hotel in Tahiti.

In 1989 he decided to embark on a political career and was elected mayor of Chaumont, in the Haute-Marne, where his grandfather had been the local deputé and later he a regional councillor for the Champagne-Ardennes.

At the same time, de Rouvre decided to further indulge his passion for motorsport and bought the AGS F1 team from its founder Henri Julien. He found some sponsorship from the electrical company Faure, built a new factory at Le Luc and hired new staff. Nothing much changed in terms of results.

In 1990 he pushed on, hired new people and found backing from fashion house Ted Lapidus, but the team was still not sufficiently competitive and suffered from the pre-qualifying arrangements at the time. De Rouvre sank $18 million of his own money into the business over the next two years, but soon had to start selling some of the 70 companies he owned to pay the bills, including Transair and the sugar refinery. Finally, unwilling to spend more, de Rouvre let AGS go into administration in 1991. It would revive with Italian money, but did not last long.

At the same time, the rival Ligier team seemed to be on the verge of an upswing. In 1990 the canny Guy Ligier used his connections with President François Mitterand to secure a Renault engine supply deal for 1992. Ligier also had funding from government companies Elf, SEITA (which owned Gitanes) and the La Française des Jeux national lottery so all was well – except the team's performance was miserable. In 1992 Guy was deeply upset when he was booed by the crowds at Monaco. He was so distressed that he decided to sell the team. By November Cyril de Rouvre had acquired 90 percent of the shares, having paid around $30 million, the money coming from a loan his film business made to him. At the time Cyril was in the process of merging the firm with its much bigger rival UGC, taking UGC shares instead of money. De Rouvre told UGC he would repay the loan by the end of the year, planning to raise the money by selling his new UGC shares, which he reckoned were worth about $30 million.

De Rouvre hired Mark Blundell and Martin Brundle to drive the Ligier-Renault JS39s, designed by Gérard Ducarouge and this resulted in several podium finishes in the course of 1993, giving the team fifth in the Constructors' Championship. It was best Ligier's result for seven years.

The problem for de Rouvre was that the UGC shares fell in value and although he delayed the sale. UGC lost patience and filed a complaint against him for fraud in May 1993. De Rouvre had to sell the shares for just $15 million and he didn't have the remaining money. The case went to court in December 1993 and De Rouvre was surprised when Judge Eva Joly decided to send Him to prison, pending an investigation. He spent two months in Fleury-Merogis jail in the south of Paris.

McLaren and Benetton immediately began looking to buy the Renault deal from him, in order to get hold of the potent V10 engines. De Rouvre wanted to sell the whole team, hoping to raise enough to pay his debts. In the end Flavio Briatore managed to get an agreement and bought the team. McLaren withdrew from the fight, unwilling to agree with some of the terms on offer. The Italian paid far less than de Rouvre had done. It was a buyer's market. The engines would be switched to Benetton in 1995 and that year Michael Schumacher won the World Championship in a Benetton-Renault. Ligier was handed over by Tom Walkinshaw at the end of 1994, although he never completed the purchase and the team was eventually sold to Alain Prost.

De Rouvre was gone from F1 after Ligier was sold and in 1995 he lost his job as mayor in the municipal elections. He went on trial on various charges in 1999, with the prosecution asking for a three-year prison sentence, a fine and a 20-year ban on running any company. He ended up with a suspended 18-month sentence, a large fine and a ban from managing a company for 3 years. Such is wealth and influence.

He turned to farming, making a brief return to politics in 2013 in the local council in Chaumont, but resigned in 2015 because he didn't like the way people treated him...

A man from the East

Paul Greifzu never took part in a Formula 1 Grand Prix, but one of his cars did. It was, in fact, the very same car in which he had been killed 15 months earlier. The Greifzu was one of the small group of post-war BMW Eigenbau Formula 2 cars, the work "eigenbau" translating literally as "home-made". They were all based on the pre-war BMW 328 sports car, using Rudolf Schleicher's potent

2-litre straight six engine, which also served as the base for the Bristol engines in the early 1950s, notably in the Cooper-Bristols.

Greifzu was not an engineer, but rather a practical amateur, who did what he could with the equipment available to him. His father owned a garage in the town of Suhl, not far from Erfurt, in Thuringia. When he was 18, after an apprenticeship as a toolmaker, Paul started working in the family garage. He soon started racing, initially with a Dixi, a German-built version of the Austin Seven. He won his first victory at Saalfeld in 1925 and then moved on to a Mercedes and a BMW motorcycle. For three years he raced with much success until a serious accident convinced him to stop. He married, worked in the family garage and started a family.

Seven years later, when the BMW 328 appeared, he decided to return to racing at the age of 33. He was one of BMW's first customers and quickly showed his abilities, notably by winning the sports car race supporting the 1938 German GP, in which he beat the factory 328s. The war then interrupted his revived career, he hid his BMW and continued to run the garage with his brother Fritz. In the course of the war the garage used forced labourers from Ukraine and when the Americans liberated Suhl in April 1945, the two brothers faced trouble, until all 12 of the workers involved protested and explained that the Greifzus had taken them from the work camp in order to save their lives and had treated them with great care and respect.

The Soviets took over the region in July that year and there was no racing for four years. Most of the car factories in the east had been destroyed or the production lines had been moved to Russia, but the BMW plant at Eisenach was revived and it began producing pre-war models under the Eisenacher Motorenwerk (EMW) banner. In July 1949, a few weeks before the Russians withdrew and the Deutsche Demokratische Republik (DDR) came into being, the first motorcycle races were held at Stralsund and Wittenberg and in September the first car race in the east place at Dessau, on a circuit which included a section of autobahn. Greifzu dusted down his 328, but it was clear that this was not competitive and so the brothers set about building their own version. This was based on a BMW 315 chassis, which was lighter than the 328. This was lowered and fitted with a 326 engine block, which EMW engineer Erich Kock mated with the light alloy cylinder heads from the 328. The bodywork was designed with the help of former Auto Union aerodynamicist Georg Hufnagel. The new car was fast and beat the other BMW Eigenbaus and the state-funded DAMWs. After a number of victories he was allowed to race in the West. The car showed promise but was destroyed when he crashed at the Nürburgring. After spending five weeks in hospital in Adenau, he returned home and built a revised version of the car. After initial wins the East Germany in 1951, he returned to the West and finished fourth at the Nürburgring. There were then further wins in the East before an international Formula 2 race at the revived Avus. The opposition was strong, with Veritas, AFM, Ferrari, Cooper and HWM (with Stirling Moss and Lance Macklin). Greifzu had prepared well. He had a special high-revving engine and gearing designed for Avus. The Greifzu was fastest in practice and after a battle with the Veritas of Toni Ulmen, Paul emerged the winner. An East German amateur had beaten the Western teams. Greifzu ended the year with another victory at the Sachsenring against a number of the Western visitors.

Greifzu turned 50 in April 1952 but was keen to go on racing. A few weeks later the racers gathered at Dessau and Greifzu was setting the pace in practice when his engine seized as he accelerated on the autobahn. It was such a violent failure that it split the engine block and the car spun out of control into a wooden fence and rolled. Greifzu was thrown out and killed. Amazingly, the damage to the car was relatively light and his widow Dora had the car rebuilt and it was entered for the German GP in 1953 for Rudolf Krause.

Greifzu remains the only driver to have won a major international single-seater race in a home-built special.

Hans and Hans

In the history of the Formula 1 World Championship there have been a variety of combinations of fathers and sons and people with the same surname but, despite the best efforts of Jacques Villeneuve, World Champion Jacques Villeneuve's uncle, to qualify for a Grand Prix, there has still been only one duo of F1 drivers with exactly the same name: Hans Stuck and his son Hans Stuck.

The first Hans fought in World War I before becoming a dairy farmer in Bavaria. He bought his first car in order to take his milk to market but he was soon taking part in hillclimbs and soon became a well known competitor. He went hunting with Julius Schrek, who was a chauffeur of a local politician. One day Schrek asked if his employer could join them and so Stuck met Adolf Hitler for the first time. At the same time he became an Austro-Daimler factory driver and on one occasion won more than a trophy at the Semmering hillclimb. The British-born Hungarian playboy Count Theodore Zichy was racing a Bugatti and bet Stuck that he would beat his Austro-Daimler. The bet was for Zichy's wife, the Scottish-born Countess Xenia. Stuck won. The relationship, however, was short as she left Stuck in 1930.

By then Austro-Daimler had withdrawn from racing and Stuck was no longer racing. Schrek recommended that Stuck talk to Hitler and he promised to help when he was in a position to do so. That happened the following year and Stuck introduced Hitler to Professor Ferdinand Porsche and showed him the designs for Porsche's revolutionary Grand Prix car, to be called an Auto Union. In 1934

Stuck enjoyed much success in the new car and stayed with the company until the war. Afterwards, he avoided the ban on German racing drivers by claiming Austrian nationality and raced in Grands Prix on several occasions for Alex von Falkenhausen's AFM team.

In the same era his son Hans was born and, thanks to the connections with Von Falkenhausen, who had become head of BMW Motorsport, Hans Jr enjoyed much success in BMW and later Ford saloons in the early 1970s. He moved into single-seaters with backing from BMW and in 1974 was second in the European Formula 2 series. He made his F1 debut that year with the March team and he continued to drive for the team on an irregular basis until 1977, while also continuing to compete for BMW in touring car racing and in IMSA. He would later switch to Brabham and looked set to win at the US Grand Prix but spun out in the wet. He moved to Shadow and then ATS before leaving F1 to begin a career in sports cars that led to a World Championship in 1985 with Rothmans Porsche and Le Mans victories in 1986 and 1987.

He won the German Touring Car Championship with Audi in 1990 and has since enjoyed life as a Volkswagen consultant, a TV commentator and as President of the Deutscher Motor Sport Bund, the country's national sporting authority.

Engines and chassis

Racing driver father and son combinations are fairly common, but engineering DNA can also pass down through the generations, although such talents are not restricted to one formula.

Take David Wood, for example. He qualified as a BSc from the celebrated Chelsea College of Aeronautical & Automotive Engineering in 1963 and was soon involved in developing the Ford BDA engine, used in Ford Escorts in rallying. The engine was later modified to be used in Formula 2 and Wood was so successful that he moved from his original workshops in a mews in London to spacious premises at Mildenhall in Suffolk, and competed successfully with the BDE engine which Dave Morgan used to win the European F2 race at Mallory Park in 1972. David Wood Engineering was in competition with Brian Hart and others in F2. It was a risky business, of course, because racing teams were notoriously bad at paying and Wood suffered badly from this.

As a result he went on to manage the engineering side of Cosworth 's F1 customer supplies, while also getting taken on by Austin Rover to help out with its Group B World Rally Championship MG Metro 6R4 programme. Originally the plan was to use the famous 3.5-litre Rover V8 (derived from a lightweight alloy GM engine). The car designer (none other than Patrick Head of Williams F1) wanted a smaller engine, so Wood reworked the Rover by lopping off two cylinders to create a 2.5-litre V6. This was a stop-gap engine while he created an all-new 90-degree V6 with 4 valves per cylinder (hence the name V64V). Rover had come late to Group B and the programme was still developing when Henri Toivonen was killed and Group B was banned.

Austin Rover quit the sport after that and the design of the V64V was sold to Tom Walkinshaw's TWR and evolved into a 3.5-litre twin-turbo engine, used in Jaguar Group C cars and in the Jaguar XJ220 road car.

Wood went back to Cosworth until 1995, after which he left the sport.

What does this have to do with F1 you might be asking? Well, David's son Ben became keen on F1 as he was growing up and studied to be an aerodynamicist. He got his first job with Minardi, before going on to have spells with Ferrari, Tyrrell, Prost, Jaguar and Minardi again before spending two years working with Piper Design on a Le Mans sports car. He then joined Super Aguri, working in the National Physical Laboratory windtunnel in Teddington, Middlesex. It was while doing this in 2008 that he began experimenting with the idea of a double diffuser. Super Aguri shut down that summer but Wood was transferred to Honda and the double diffuser concept was built into the 2009 Honda F1 car. At this point the Japanese firm made a really bad decision and quit F1, giving the team (and some money to run it) to Ross Brawn and other members of the team management. The rest is history. Brawn secured Mercedes engines and in 2009 Brawn GP won the World Championship with Jenson Button... By the time the other teams had caught up, it was too late.

Wood today runs his own aerodynamic firm called Dynamique Ltd, with its own wind tunnel near Oxford. It does contract engineering - but doesn't say for whom. The word is that the Ford GT might have received some input from the firm. Wood also runs another business called Anakata Wind Energy, which markets small-scale wind turbines, using F1 aerodynamic expertise...

Naming engines

Can you imagine what would happen today if an executive in a big insurance company proposed that the firm bankroll a Formula 1 engine programme - in order to promote a computer leasing subsidiary? It doesn't sound very likely, does it? Except that it happened...

The United States Fidelity and Guaranty Company, an insurance company, set up shop in Baltimore in 1896 and soon became one of the country's biggest such firms, surviving ups and downs and gradually building up. In the early 1980s, the then chairman and CEO Jack Moseley transformed the business into a holding company, renamed it USF&G and went on a buying spree. The company had annual revenues of $4.3 billion and profits of around $300 million and so money was not a problem. USF&G collected real estate, bonds and companies, some of them unrelated to the insurance industry. One such business was a Detroit-based computer leasing company called Megatron Inc., which had been established in 1977 by an enterprising individual call John J Schmidt.

Schmidt was a huge fan of racing and managed to convince USF&G that it ought to be in F1, primarily as a way to do business, by bringing top executives of big corporations to watch the races, to promote its asset management activities. For 1986 USF&G was talked into becoming the title sponsor of the Arrows-BMW F1 team, which was run by team bosses Jackie Oliver and Alan Rees. The money helped the team to grow and matters were helped by the implosion of the Haas Lola F1 team, which provided Arrows with the chance to hire a young designer called Ross Brawn.

At the same time, BMW decided to quit F1, which meant that its customer teams needed to find alternative engines. Benetton jumped to Ford while Oliver decided on a different strategy and set out to buy the engine programme from BMW, to help the Munich firm recoup some of its investment. He then took on engine tuner Heini Mader to prepare and develop the BMW 4-cylinder turbos and the engines were paid for by USF&G and badged as Megatrons. The costs were partially offset by selling engines to Ligier.

The Arrows-Megatron A10 was a relatively successful car with the team finishing sixth in the Constructors' World Championship in 1987. Brawn then reworked it as the A10B and Arrows finished fourth in the Constructors' Championship, it's best ever result, in 1988. The rules were changing in 1989 with turbos being banned and Arrows switched to Cosworth power. The team slipped back to seventh in the Constructors', Brawn was lured away to design Jaguar sports cars and USF&G withdrew. It was in trouble. Large losses saw Moseley replaced by Norman Blake, who took radical steps to save the business. He sold off the non-core business, fired half the staff and tripled the company's share price. By 1998 he was able to sell the business to the Saint Paul Companies for $2.8 billion.

Little brothers

James Stewart was born in the village of Milton, on the banks of the River Clyde, not far from Dumbarton, in 1931. His father Bob was the son of the head gamekeeper on the Eaglesham estate, owned by the Weir family, in Renfrewshire. As a youngster Bob had worked as a draughtsman with the Weir family's engineering company at Cathcart in Glasgow and had raced motorcycles as an amateur, but then in 1928 he set up a garage near Dumbarton and secured a concession to sell Austins and later Jaguars.

James, known as Jimmy – like the Hollywood star – grew up surrounded by automobiles and regularly tested customers' cars on the roads around nearby Loch Lomond. When he was 17 he acquired a MGTD roadster and he began to compete in local hillclimbs. After a couple of years in different machines, he managed to convince his father that he ought to buy a Jaguar C-Type so that Jimmy could join Edinburgh businessman David Murray in a new sports car team called Ecurie Ecosse. As a result in 1952 Jimmy Stewart became a rising star on the British scene, although his career was disrupted somewhat because of National Service, during which he served with the Royal Electrical & Mechanical Engineers (REME).

Once that was done he resumed his career and in 1953 Ecurie Ecosse entered him for the British Grand Prix at the wheel of a Cooper-Bristol. He qualified 15th and was running sixth in the closing laps, in the wet, when he spun off.

He continued to be successful in Ecurie Ecosse sports cars but in the summer of 1954 at Le Mans, while driving a factory Aston Martin DB3S coupé, which he was sharing with Graham Whitehead, he suffered a fractured elbow when the car went out of control at Maison Blanche during the seventh hour of the race. He was thrown out and slid down the grass verge, watching his car somersaulting to destruction. He was out for the rest of the season but returned with an Ecurie Ecosse Jaguar D-type in 1955.

He did well, but at the Nurburgring suffered a brake failure and crashed into an earth bank, the car flipped upside down, trapping him inside, obscured from the track by a thick hedge. Fortunately, 10 minutes later Stirling Moss arrived and spotted the tyre marks and stopped and was able to release Stewart from the car. He had broken his arm again.

His mother wanted him to stop racing and when warned that another fracture might permanently damage his arm, he took the decision to retire from racing. He was just 24. He went back to the family garage. His younger brother, eight years his junior, was encouraged to take up clay pigeon shooting. But then one day, quite by chance, young Jackie Stewart discovered car racing…

Father and son

In Grand Prix racing history, there have been two Henri Durands, both from the town of Mamazet, near the celebrated fortified city of Carcassonne, in the south of France. Unsurprisingly, Henri Sr was the father of Henri Jr -but both have had very different paths in the sport.

Henri Sr was a racing driver, born in 1903, who joined the happy band of daredevils who raced in France in the 1920s and 1930s. He started out with a Rally cyclecar, powered by a SCAP engine, but soon moved on to acquire a more potent two-litre Bugatti T35, a Grand Prix car that allowed him to race against the big names of the day. It was underpowered by the time he acquired the car in the early 1930s and he would later switch to a Bugatti T37, a 1.5-litre version of the T35, designed for voiturette racing, which gave him a better chance of success. He would race throughout the 1930s, his best results coming in Casablanca in 1932, where he finished second in the voiturette class at Anfa to Pierre Veyron (after whom the modern Bugatti is named) and later a third place at Albi in 1934 and second (to Veyron again) at the same track the following year.

He then faded away from the racing scene and the name Henri Durand did not pop up again until the 1980s, when his son Henri Jr, born in 1960, emerged as the leading light of the generation of French aerodynamicists, trained at the Ecole Nationale Superieure de l'Aeronautique et de l'Espace in Toulouse, who joined the sport in the 1980s.

F1 teams had begun to understand how important aerodynamics are for racing cars, largely as a result of grand-effect machinery, pioneered by Lotus in the late 1970s. It was still a fairly hit-and-miss business at the start and Ligier's success in the 1979-1981 period was more to do with practical knowledge than science. When the team realised that it needed a different approach it went looking for aerodynamicists and signed up the 23-year-old Durand to work on the Renault-powered JS23, which had been designed by Michel Beaujon and Claude Galopin. This was not too bad, scoring some points in the hands of Andrea de Cesaris, but the JS25, which followed in 1985, was better and scored four podium finishes in the hands of Jacques Laffite and Philippe Streiff. The

JS27 of 1986 helped the team to finish fifth in the Constructors' Championship, the team's best showing since its glory days.

Sadly, the collaboration with Renault ended and the team went into a dive and Durand was lured away to work with John Barnard at Ferrari. This partnership resulted in the radical but elegant Ferrari 639 and 640 designs - the predecessors of the 641, one of which features today in the Museum of Modern Art in New York.

The 640 won its first race in the hands of Nigel Mansell in Brazil in 1989 but Ferrari decided to change its approach and Barnard was pushed out and Durand departed soon afterwards, the Frenchman joining McLaren in the summer of 1990. He replaced Mike Gascoyne as the head of aerodynamics and remained at McLaren for the next 10 years, becoming a UK citizen along the way.

The team won the World Championship in 1998 and 1999 with Mika Hakkinen. At the end of 2000, however, he decided to return to return to France to become Technical Director of Prost Grand Prix. That was not a great success because Prost never had the money to do the job properly and Durand moved on to Jordan, where he became director of race and test engineering before being taken on by Red Bull Cheever Racing in Indycar in 2004. He would return to Europe later to work briefly with the abortive Epsilon F1 team in to Vitoria-Gasteiz, in northern Spain before getting a job with Mecachrome back in the US market. He spent a while working with Panther Racing in the Indy Racing League before finally settling into a job at Toyota Racing Development in Charlotte, NC.

Durand was nonetheless a competitor, like his father, but his preferred sport was rowing, right back to his college days when he competed at national level. In recent years, Durand suffered a serious surfing accident, which resulted in his left leg being amputated below the knee. Keen to continue rowing, but unable to find a prosthetic leg which could do the job, he solved the problem by designing one himself, which was then machined from solid titanium by the Joe Gibbs Racing NASCAR team. This allowed him to return to competition in rowing and to inspire others with disabilities to chase their dreams.

The godfather

Charles Pic became a Formula 1 driver because of a gift his godfather gave him on his 12th birthday, back in 2002. A go kart. He was soon competing successfully in events around his home town of Montélimar, in the Drome département, between Lyon and Avignon. His brother Arthur followed him into the sport.

Montélimar is famous for its nougat and because it sits beside the A7 motorway, known as the Autoroute du Soleil, which links the north of France with Provence. It was this strategic location that led Charles's great-grandfather Charles André to pick Montélimar as the headquarters for his transport company, which was originally based in the more remote Ardeche.

From the start, André specialised in transporting petrol from the refineries in Marseille to garages across the country. Groupe Charles André Transports (otherwise known as GCAtrans) is one of Europe's largest transport firms and owns a string of other businesses, notably the Golf de la Valdaine in Montélimar, a hotel/golf complex and the Les Barmes de l'Ours resort at Val d'Isere, in the Alps.

When you own thousands of trucks, many of them fuel tankers, finding sponsorship is not such a difficult business. This meant that it was fairly easy for Pic to find money and his talent took him through the junior formulae and he arrived in F1 with Marussia in 2012. He would move on to Caterham in 2013 and became a Lotus test driver in 2014. His brother Arthur has raced in GP2 for the last three seasons and is still hoping to find a way to follow Charles into F1.

The family empire is today presided over by their mother Delphine André, the grand-daughter of the founder. She has run the business since her two boys were babies, having taken over the firm after the early death of her father Charles-Pierre in 1991. Before that, in the 1980s, when Delphine was a teenager, GCAtrans agreed to help the fuel company Elf with sponsorship of the Winfield Racing team in the French Formula 3 Championship. As a result, Delphine got to know the Winfield Racing drivers. She married GCAtrans managing-director, Jean-Christophe Pic, and when Charles arrived she asked one of her racing friends to be Charles's godfather. Eric Bernard was by then a Formula 1 driver, having risen from Winfield Racing to F1 by 1989.

Small wonder he chose a go-kart as a birthday present for young Charles…

Friends

The name Jean-Claude Guénard is not widely known in Formula 1 these days and if you Google him, you will find that most of the mentions are about his death, in August 1987, alongside Didier Pironi and Bernard Giroux in their Colibri-sponsored offshore powerboat during the Needles Trophy race off the Isle of Wight. A couple of weeks earlier they had won the Arendal race in

Norway and were running in second place, battling with the Italian boat Pinot di Pinot, piloted by Renato della Valle. As they approached one of the turning points on the course the Colibri hit the wake of a 37,000-ton oil tanker that was passing nearby. The lightweight boat flew into the air, flipped over and crashed upside-down onto the surface of the water, still travelling at high speed. The three men were killed. The headlines the next day talked of Pironi and Guénard and Giroux became footnotes in history, which was not really fair, as both had led extraordinary lives. Giroux was a rally co-driver, who had won several events with Bernard Darniche. He had become a TV star and was also a two-time winner of the Paris-Dakar, once as co-driver to René Metge in 1981 and once alongside Ari Vatanen in 1987.

Guénard was an equally impressive character. His relationship with Pironi went back to the 1969, when the 16-year-old Didier wanted to become a member of Guénard's Kawasaki motorcycle team in the 24-hour Bol d'Or race at Montlhéry. Pironi's mother stopped that happening...

Guénard was 10 years older than Pironi and had begun his racing career in his late teens and in 1963, when he was 20, he won the French 250cc National Championship and finished fourth in a one-off entry in the French GP. Along with Patrick Depailler, he would be a protege of Jean-Pierre Beltoise, and part of a group of motorcycle racers who lived in the southern suburbs of Paris.

Like many motorcycle racers at the time, the lure of car racing was strong and, while he continued to race books, he moved into Formula 3 as well with a variety of different machinery, beginning with a Matra, followed by a Tecno and an Alpine. He did well and among his team-mates in the era were Jean-Pierre Jarier and Jean-Luc Salomon, both rising stars at the time. He also raced an Alfa Romeo for Conrero in French touring car events, with Depailler as his team mate. He would also compete in a few rallies, notably the 1971 Tour de France which he did with Jean-Pierre Jabouille in a Ferrari, and finished second. He later shared an Alpine with Bob Wollek in a European event.

By 1971, however, he did not have the money to make further progress in racing and decided to retire and concentrate on motorsport engineering, working with Jabouille in Formula 3, along with a young mechanic called Jacques Laffite and the Alpine engine expert Bernard Dudot. Depailler, Jabouille's Alpine team-mate, won the title that year with Jabouille third. The next step was Formula 2, which he did with the support of Elf, using a variety of machinery before getting this hands on the renamed Alpine A367, which was badged as the Elf 2. In 1976, with backing from Elf Switzerland, and aerodynamic help from Marcel Hubert, Guénard reworked the car as the Elf 2J and Jabouille won the European Formula 2 title.

This same group then began working on the Alpine-Renault A500 project, the secret F1 car that would eventually become the basis of the RS01. It was not until January 1977 that Renault admitted that it had an F1 programme and

Guénard was named as the project leader on the chassis side. The car began testing in June and made its debut at the British GP and for the next two years the team worked its way through a plethora of problems, largely engine-related before results started to come, culminating with the team's first victory at the French GP in July 1979.

Jabouille and René Arnoux would win three races in 1980 before Jabouille crashed heavily in Canada and broke his leg. He would move to Ligier in 1981 and Guénard went with him. Jabouille's injury meant that he could no longer drive and so the two men worked closely with Laffite in the years that followed before Guy Ligier asked Guénard to become the project leader of the Ligier Indycar, which appeared in 1984. Unfortunately the money promised for the project did not appear and the operation was closed down before the car could be developed and so Guénard went off to work with Pironi's Leader Boats company. At the same time, he and Jabouille created another business, preparing Lada Nivas for the Paris-Dakar Rally, with three cars entered for Jabouille, Jean-Louis Schlesser and Pierre Lartigue, with funding from Pastis 51.

Guénard's desire to compete led him to becoming the throttle man with Pironi…

Jean-Claude Guénard is buried in the cemetery of Saint Pierre et Saint Charles in Villeneuve-le-Roi.

Two of a kind

If you find yourself in Monaco, go down to the port, just behind the swimming pool and you will find a bust of Louis Chiron, Monaco's most famous Grand Prix driver. He was born in the town in 1899, the son of a hotel worker who would rise to become the maitre d'hotel at the Hotel de Paris. The good-looking Louis found work a professional dancer, twirling lonely wealthy women around the dance floor. He was keen to become a racing driver and thanks to the support of a wealthy American lady he was able to get his hands on a Brescia Bugatti in 1923. One can only imagine what she got in exchange for this generous gesture.

At the same time Mariette Delangle was doing something very similar. The daughter of a postman, she was born in 1900 and grew up into a very attractive young woman. She became a professional dancer, using the name Hélène Nice, which she would later shorten to Hellé Nice. Some of her dancing was deemed to be "exotic" and there are some revealing photographs of her in her youth, which leave very little to the imagination. She was as keen as Chiron to become a racing driver and she achieved her goal by becoming "friends" with

Baron Philippe de Rothschild, of the celebrated banking family. She was given a Bugatti Type 35 by the playboy baron.

Chiron had moved on by then and his career was being supported by Alfred Hoffmann, heir to the Hoffmann-La Roche pharmaceutical fortune. Chiron would later become the lover of Hoffman's wife Alice, which ended up with him being fired and the Hoffmans divorcing.

Once established, both Chiron and Hellé Nice enjoyed successful careers in racing in the 1930s. Neither married and Alice Hoffman left Chiron and eventually married the German driver Rudolf Caracciola instead. Hellé Nice also made friends with the Germans, being the lover of Baron Huschke Von Hanstein.

After World War II, Chiron denounced Hellé Nice as having been a collaborator during the war. He offered no evidence to support his claim, although it is clear that before the war she had been friends with Von Hanstein, who raced BMWs, sponsored by the SS…

There seems to be nothing more to it than that. This denunciation destroyed Hellé Nice's career as her sponsors immediately stopped supporting her, on the basis that Chiron could not have simply made the story up. No-one really knows why Chiron did what he did. Perhaps it was just because they were too alike…

The suave Louis went on to become the oldest F1 driver ever when he raced in the 1955 Monaco Grand Prix – at the age of 55.

The power of practical engineering

It is a story which began in Castlemaine, Victoria, an old Australian gold mining town, about 75 miles to the northwest of Melbourne. Robert Russell, a Irish immigrant who had become a school inspector, lost his wife of 11 years. Two years later, in 1891, he married again, his new wife Lucy being 14 years his junior. They had a son almost immediately and he was named Robert, after his father. As he was growing up in Geelong he became known as Geoff, Geoffrey being his middle name. He served an apprenticeship and became a motor mechanic, settling in Wangaratta, a town on the Melbourne-Sydney highway, about 150 miles from Melbourne.

When he was 23, Geoff Russell enlisted in the Australian Imperial Force and was sent off to serve with a field ambulance unit at Gallipoli and on the Western Front. He returned to Australia as a sergeant in 1919 and, once demobbed, he bought a share of the garage in Wangaratta.

But things had changed and after two years he sold out and moved to Melbourne to be his own boss, starting a small business reconditioning engines, in a tin shed in Collingwood. Russell was a practical engineer. He didn't say a lot but he was an excellent craftsman. It was a good time to be in the car business as vehicle sales in Australia boomed. He and a colleague called Bill Ryan spotted an opportunity as many of the cars in Australia were imported. They were expensive and new parts were subject to tariffs and long delays. So they decided to manufacture parts. The company was called Replacement Parts Pty Ltd, but it soon became known as Repco.

The Great Depression had little effect on Repco because people in Australia stopped buying new cars and instead repaired their old ones, which meant that Repco was kept busy. By the end of the 1930s, Russell was wealthy enough to buy out Ryan and he then floated the company on the Melbourne stock exchange, remaining as the largest shareholder and staying on as managing director.

Sadly, Russell died of a brain tumour in 1946, but his company lived on and in the same year one of his engineers, Charlie Dean, acquired a Maybach engine which had been taken from an abandoned armoured car and shipped back to Australia by the government. After it had been thoroughly examined it was sold to Dean who modified it for racing. The result was the Maybach Special Mk1, which was raced in the years that followed by Stan Jones, often beating the imported racing machinery. Its triumphs included the 1954 New Zealand Grand Prix at Ardmore.

Realising the advertising value of the sport Repco became involved in the sport as the business began to expand internationally, supporting Jack Brabham. In 1961 he set up Motor Racing Developments Ltd in Repco premises in Surbiton, England and began building his own cars. Many of the early ones were known as Repco Brabhams.

At the end of 1964, the FIA decided the engine formula should change in 1966. At the time there were six principal teams in F1: Ferrari, Honda and BRM all built their own engines, while Lotus, Brabham and Cooper all used the Coventry Climax engine. It was, therefore, a major shock when Climax announced that it was quitting the sport, early in 1965. This meant that teams had less than 10 months to find new engines. Lotus decided to go with BRM, Cooper did a deal with Maserati but Brabham, ever the practical engineer, decided that there was a better solution and suggested to Repco CEO Charles McGrath that he might like to fund a project to turn an aluminium V8 Oldsmobile engine, abandoned by GM because of the production costs involved, into a F1 engine.

Brabham had seen the engine in action in the Sandown Park International race in 1962 where Chuck Daigh's Scarab ran with a Buick version of the engine. The same year Dan Gurney had used one at Indianapolis in the Mickey Thompson Harvey Aluminum Special. Jack bought one and shipped it to Australia to allow Repco's chief engineer Frank Hallam to take a look. Hallam took on Phil Irving to oversee the project at the Repco Engine Laboratory in Richmond, Victoria. The redesign of the engine was completed by Irving in a rented flat in London.

It made its F1 debut in South Africa in January 1966. Jack gave Repco its first win in the International Trophy in May that year and won the French GP in July, the first of four wins which took him to the World Championship.

The following year Repco did its own castings and an improved version of the engine took Denny Hulme to a second title. By then, however, the opposition was reacting and the arrival of the Cosworth DFV meant that Repco had to upgrade again in 1968. It was not a great success, although Jochen Rindt used one to finish third at the Nurburgring. At the end of 1968 Repco decided that the programme was too expensive and Brabham switched to Cosworth engines. Repco remained in racing, producing Repco-Holden Formula 5000 engines through until the late 1970s, but its F1 adventure was over...

Take a fire pump...

In 1950, the British Government asked engineering firms to create a new generation portable fire-fighting device that could pump 350 gallons of water a minute at 100 psi and yet still be carried easily by two men. It was challenge. The previous units had pumped half as much and had weighed twice as much.

The fork lift truck manufacturing company Coventry Climax decided to bid for the contract and a new pump was designed by Walter Hassan and Harry Mundy, both of whom had worked in the automobile industry before the war. The result was the Feather Weight Pump (FWP), which won Coventry Climax a large government contract.

Racing people are inventive and always on the lookout for engines with a good power-to-weight ratio. The FWP was spotted and racing people began to push the company to enlarge the design to 1100cc. These were called Feather Weight Automotive (FWA) engines and were first used in Kieft sports cars at Le Mans in 1954. Stretched to 1.5-litres they became the dominant engines in Formula 2 and it was not long before the first Coventry Climaxes began appearing in F1, powering Coopers. Stirling Moss won the first F1 victory in a 2-litre Cooper-Climax in Argentina in 1958.

Families of engines

Engines are funny things. They can be used in many different ways and can be called by many different names - even if they are fundamentally the same. General Motors began experimenting with lightweight aluminium engines in the early 1950s, at a time when Alcoa, the Aluminum Company of America, was pushing for automakers to use more aluminium. In 1950 Charles Chayne, Buick's chief engineer, decided that the company should design an experimental high-performance aluminum V8 and Joseph Turlay, who had been with the firm since 1929 and was then its chief engine designer, set to work to create such an engine. The engine displaced 3.5-litres or 215 cubic inches. It weighed 550 lbs and produced 335 hp, very impressive figures in that era. After being used in various concept cars, the engine was developed for production in the late 1950s, and nearly a million such engine would be produced in the early 1960s for Buick and Oldsmobile models. The problem was that casting aluminium was difficult and the engines suffered from porosity problems, which caused serious oil leaks and while it was the basis of the very successful cast iron V6 engine, known as the Fireball, the aluminium versions were dropped after 1963. In 1964, with GM not having the patience to redesign the power unit, the engine was sold to Rover in the UK. However the power-to-weight ratio was such that the racing fraternity was interested in the engine and Mickey Thompson entered a stock-block Buick 215-powered car in the 1962 Indianapolis 500 and Dan Gurney qualified eighth before retiring with transmission problems. Rover used the engines in a variety of models and, at one point, GM even tried to buy it back, but Rover declined the offer. Before the engine was sold it was used in various Buick, Oldmobile and Pontiac models and surplus engine blocks were picked up by racers and used in various different ways. It was used by Bruce McLaren in the Zerex Special, which he has acquired from Roger Penske in 1964, while Jack Brabham used a version of the same engine, redesigned and developed by Repco as the basis for the Repco V8, with which he won the World Championship in 1966 and 1967. Later the same design was used in racing versions of the Rover V8.

An engine called Martin

If you mention the words Ted and Martin in relation to Formula 1 these days, most people will think about the Sky TV presenters Ted Kravitz and Martin Brundle. Back in the 1970s, Ted Martin was an engine designer.

Edward C Martin was an RAF pilot during World War II and then became involved in the design of model engines with the Anchor Motor Company in Chester in the late 1940s. In 1952 he moved to Canada to work with GM and worked there for the next 17 years, although he also established a UK company called Alexander Engineering to tune Formula Junior engines. He then developed his own four cylinder 1500cc Martin FJ engine and when F1 changed to the 3-litre formula in 1966,it seemed logical to combine two of these to create a three-litre V8. The first such engines were run in a modified Lotus 35 chassis, prepared by John Pearce, a wheel manufacturer, who ran a garage specialising in racing conversions, in the west London suburb of Southall.

Pearce had started out as a welder at Peerless Cars Ltd in Slough, a small sports car company which duly went bust in the late 1950s. It was revived making a car called the Warwick, but this too went out of business and so Pearce moved on to the Cooper Car Company in Surbiton and then joined Chris Lawrence's LawrenceTune in Acton. At the same time Pearce operated a spares business using an old double-decker bus, which was parked on old railway land in Staines. When he had sufficient money, in 1962, he bought the garage at 10-12 Western Road, Southall and began manufacturing magnesium alloy wheels, sold under the JAP Magna brand.

The Pearce-run Lotus-Martin was raced at the start of 1966 by Roy Pike and finished third in a race at Mallory Park, but the following year it proved to be slow in practice for the Race of Champions, despite being driven by Piers Courage. He later crashed in testing at Snetterton and the project was abandoned. That season Pearce ran a Cooper-Ferrari for Chris Lawrence and he took fifth in the Gold Cup at Oulton Park.

Martin commuted backwards and forwards between the UK and Canada, so development work on his V8 was slow, but Pearce pushed ahead with his own chassis, while the Cooper-Ferrari was raced again in the British and German GPs. The Pearce-Martin proper appeared in January 1967, at the Racing Car Show at Olympia. The first of the cars was tested at Brands Hatch but was destroyed by Lawrence, who was pushing hard to try to beat a time set by Tony

Lanfranchi in the Cooper-Ferrari.

The team built another chassis and was scheduled to make its debut at the International Trophy at Silverstone at the end of April, with two Pearce-Martins entered for American Earl Jones and Lanfranchi, with Robin Darlington entered in the Cooper-Ferrari. On the night before practice began the team's transporter caught fire and everything was destroyed.

Pearce and Martin went their separate ways after that with Pearce's business shutting down in 1973, also apparently after a fire. Pearce turned to farming and settled near Maidenhead.

Martin designed engines for various projects, including the Monica sports car in 1973 before returning to his first love, model engineering in his retirement. Dreams don't always come true.

Another Russian tale

Odessa is a beautiful place. It became part of Russia after the two Russo-Turkish Wars of the late 18th Century. It was a warm water port, something Russia needed, and Catherine the Great ordered a new city to be built. Much of its development was overseen by French exiles, who had fled the Revolution in 1789. In 1815 Odessa was declared a free port, in order to boost trade. It quickly became a cosmopolitan and rich city where, according to Alexander Pushkin, the air was "filled with all Europe, French is spoken and there are European papers and magazines to read". The city had a huge Jewish population, up to 35 percent of the citizens, and this led to troubles from time to time when anti-Semitic Russians attacked and killed Jews.

Joseph Poberejsky was Jewish, born in Odessa in 1885. His family seems to have been wealthy and he was a member of the city's financial elite. This allowed him to work as an inventor. With the arrival of electricity there were plenty of new ideas to be developed.

The Russian Revolution in 1917 threw the country into chaos and many of Odessa's rich decided to leave, in fear of the Bolsheviks. Poberejsky was 32 and he headed for Paris, where at least he could speak the language. He settled in the comfortable 16th arrondissement and began using the name Jacques in order to integrate more. He would eventually become a naturalised French citizen. He continued to invent and also acquired the rights to the inventions of others. Automobiles and aviation created new opportunities and he patented flexible hoses which could withstand vibration and a self-sealing fuel tank. There was also a water heater for farms so that animals could get water in freezing conditions. The profits he made by licensing the inventions were invested in real estate and in new ideas. He was keen on cars and bought a Rolls Royce which he had re-bodied in a much sportier fashion by the Binder carriage-building firm on the Boulevard Haussmann.

Jacques soon moved his growing family into a mansion in exclusive Neuilly-sur-Seine. But when the war came in 1939 the family, fearing persecution, sailed to America and settled in affluent Westchester County, just outside New York. They returned to Paris after the war ended and Jacques built a new car which he intended to sell. It was a Rolls Royce with his own Carrosserie Poberejsky bodywork. It was unveiled at the Geneva Motor Show in 1949. Rolls Royce threatened legal action…

Jacques died later that year at the age of 64, leaving his fortune to his son Michel, who was then 19. Fascinated by automobiles, the youngster was a regular visitor to Gaston Docime's Bugatti garage in Neuilly and the garage owner decided to take him under his wing. In 1950 they visited the Lamberjack garage in the rue Bayen, in the 17th arrondissement, and Poberejsky was convinced to buy a unique 1938 Bugatti Atalante 57SC, the only supercharged Atalante produced by the factory, although many other Atalantes had superchargers added by their owners.

He soon began racing the car at Montlhéry, using the pseudonym "Mike Sparken". He enjoyed racing and soon acquired Aston Martin DB2 and DB3 sports cars, which he re-bodied before moving on to a Ferrari 750 Monza. He won occasional races and was considered a very decent driver. In 1955 "Mike Sparken" shared his Ferrari with Masten Gregory at Le Mans – although the pair suffered an engine failure early on.

Poberejsky was then 25 and keen to try Grand Prix racing and so did a deal with Amedée Gordini to race a factory Gordini in the British Grand Prix at Aintree. He qualified 23rd and drove a solid race to finish seventh, despite a clutch failure. It was a pretty good effort. For whatever reason, however, he then decided to stop racing, although he continued to deal in interesting automobiles for the rest of his days. He was the owner of a number of extraordinary machines, including a second Bugatti Atalante and, most impressively, an Alfa Romeo Alfetta Grand Prix car, which he prised from the factory by offering them the streamlined 1938 Alfa Romeo 8C 2900B which had shone at Le Mans in the hands of Clemente Biondetti and Raymond Sommer. Alfa Romeo wanted that car and the Alfetta was in a poor state. It was the only Alfetta to ever get into private hands.

Poberejsky moved from Neuilly to Cap Ferrat on the Cote d'Azur as he grew older. In the end he was diagnosed with cancer. He died in 2012 at the age of 82.

A small world

The motorsport community in Finland is a small world. It's a huge country, covering 130,000 square miles but has a population of only 5.5 million, the majority live in the south of the country, where the climate is harsh – as opposed to the north where it is brutal.

Mika Hakkinen grew up in the suburbs of Helsinki. When he was six his father bought him a kart, acquired from a 21-year-old called Henri Toivonen, who was about to switch from circuit racing to rallying. Henri would soon become the youngest driver ever to win a World Championship Rally.

When Mika was old enough to start racing, he found that his primary rival was a youngster who lived on the same street as he did: Mika Salo. Hakkinen attended the Linnanmäen Sirkuskoulu, a circus school in Helsinki, while also honing his driving skills by driving a VW Beetle on a frozen lake with another pal, Mika Sohlberg, who went on to be a World Rally Championship driver.

When Hakkinen graduated to Formula Ford he bought his first car from a youngster called JJ Lehto and then one day went to a sauna and bumped into Keke Rosberg, who agreed to be his manager. Hakkinen and Salo both ended up in British F3 in 1990, the pair dominating the series: Hakkinen won nine of the 17 races and Salo won six. As they say in Disneyland, It's a small world…

How to kidnap a World Champion

It may be that one day, in the not-too-distant future, motor racing will return to Cuba, now that Fidel Castro has finally died. The sport visited Havana in the 1950s, but it did not end well. At the time Havana was a magnificent den of vice, where Hollywood stars, socialites, debutantes and American mobsters would go to have a good time. The rich jet-setters required luxury hotels, restaurants, night clubs, golf clubs and casinos and the rich Cubans join in the fun. The problem was that there were not many of them. Most of the population was poor. It didn't help that the government of Fulgencio Batista was woefully corrupt and authoritarian, but motor racing has often turned a blind eye to such things and so a decent field was found for a sports car race which the Cubans hoped would draw attention to their country and attract more visitors.

A street circuit was laid out along the Malecon, the broad boulevard that ran along the seafront, with a pit area located in the shadow of the Hotel Nacional. Although the cars were not Formula 1 machines, they did attract some of the top drivers of the day, notably Juan Manuel Fangio, and he won won the first event at the wheel of a Maserati 300, leading home Carroll Shelby and Alfonso de Portago. The racers were joined by Hollywood star Gary Cooper, while de Portago brought along his new girlfriend, actress Linda Christian, who had only recently split up with Tyrone Power. There was huge local interest in the event, not least because of a lottery offering the first prize of a Cadillac and a ticket to visit Monza for the Italian Grand Prix.

The following year there were bigger and better plans with the race scheduled for Monday, February 24, with the usual practice and qualifying during the weekend. On the Sunday night Fangio emerged from the lift in the foyer of the Hotel Lincoln, in Havana's old town, planning to have dinner with Alejandro de Tomaso and Maserati team director Nello Ugolini. A man in a leather jacket approached, showed Fangio an automatic pistol and told him not to say or do anything. At first the World Champion thought it was a joke, but he then agreed to follow the kidnapper Oscar Lucero to a car waiting outside. The team of nine kidnappers vanished into the night with the World Champion.

The aim was to raise the profile of the Cuban Revolution without doing anyone any serious harm. Batista's security forces spent the night scouring the city, looking for Fangio, hoping to find him before the race. The next morning, Faustino Perez, the man in charge of Castro's clandestine operations, arrived in Havana and met Fangio, apologising for the kidnapping and explaining that he would be released after the race.

The race was delayed 90 minutes, in the hope that Fangio would reappear, but eventually it had to go ahead. There was a huge crowd and this proved to be a problem because on the seventh lap the Cuban driver Armando Garcia Cifuentes lost control of his Ferrari exiting a corner by the American Embassy and ploughed into the crowd, killing seven people and injuring 40. The race was stopped and Stirling Moss was declared the winner. Fangio was duly released and told the media that he had been treated well. The kidnap was such big news that CBS paid Fangio to fly to New York to appear on the Ed Sullivan Show. The irony was not missed by Fangio, who remarked that five World Championship had not been enough to get him on the show...

There was, however, a darker side to the story. Two months later Lucero was arrested by Batista's secret police. He was interrogated for several weeks for information about his operations and then he was shot. Today he is one of the heroes of the Cuban Revolution and a university is named in his honour.

Fangio did not return to Cuba until 1981 when he went as an envoy of Mercedes-Benz to conclude a deal with the Castro government for a supply of trucks. Two of the kidnappers, notably Perez, were by then government ministers… Castro interrupted a meeting to greet the old racing driver, who had unwittingly helped the revolution.

Maserati versus Maserati

The Fiat-owned luxury car company, unveiled a concept car called the Alfieri. It was named after the man who had established the Maserati company 100 years earlier.

It is a story which began in the 1880s when Rodolfo Maserati, a railway engineer, began a family. There were seven sons, although one died as an infant. The oldest Carlo had built his own engine when he was 17 and he was soon hired by Fiat. He moved on to rival Isotta Fraschini at 22 and was soon joined in the company by his younger brother Alfieri, who was then in his teens. Carlo went on to become the manager of the Junior company in Milan, and took on his 14-year-old brother Ettore in 1908. Two years later Alfieri was joined at Isotta Fraschini by his older brother Bindo. The same year Carlo contracted tuberculosis and died at 29.

In 1913 Alfieri opened a garage in Bologna, in order to service Isotta Fraschinis. The following year he decided to go a step further and registered the Officine Alfieri Maserati. He was joined by Ettore. They then recruited 16-year-old Ernesto, the youngest of the brothers, while Mario, the only brother not interested in cars, was asked to use his artistic talents to create a logo for the new business. World War I broke out soon afterwards and Alfieri and Ettore were called up, leaving Ernesto to work in the garage.

The business did not really take off until 1920 when the brothers were reunited and Alfieri built a racing car with an Isotta Fraschini frame, fitted with a Hispano Suiza engine. The car soon began winning races and in 1922 the brothers began working with Diatto with the plan of building a Grand Prix car but the company did not have the money. The brothers, with the backing of Marquis Diego de Sterlich, who sold 750 acres of land to pay for the investment, bought 10 Diatto 30 Sport chassis, and used these to produce the first cars to carrying the Maserati badge.

They were followed in 1926 by the Maserati Tipo 26, based on the Grand Prix design they had envisaged. The car made its debut in the Targa Florio of 1926 and won its class, and soon there was demand for customer cars. Alfieri was seriously injured in an accident in 1927 but success followed with the Tipo 26M with which Luigi Arcangeli winning the Reale Premio di Roma in 1930. In 1932, however, Alfieri died from complications caused by his accident, at the age of only 44. Bindo left Isotta Fraschini and joined Ettore and Ernesto to run the company. More success followed with Tazio Nuvolari winning the 1933 Belgian Grand Prix with the Maserati 8CM and with the voiturette Maserati 6CM.

The rise of the German Grand Prix teams in 1934 and 1935 led the brothers to the realization that they would not remain successful without serious industrial support and they negotiated a deal in 1936 to sell the business to steel baron Adolfo Orsi, beginning in January 1937. They agreed to stay with the company for a period of 10 years. There would be a new Grand Prix car, called the 4CL in 1939 and success at Indianapolis in 1939 and 1940 with the 8CTF and in the latter year Orsi moved the firm to Modena. There was little racing after that. The Orsis built trucks during the war and then went back to building road cars in the post-war era. They handed over the racing activities to Scuderia Milano.

In January 1947 when their contracts with Orsi expired the Maserati Brothers departed to form a new company called Officine Specializzate Costruzione Automobili (OSCA), back in Bologna. In the post-war period they build small sports cars, some of which were converted to Formula 2 spec, and in 1951 they built a new 4.5-litre V12 engine, which was raced in a Maserati chassis by Prince Bira. The car won its first race at Goodwood in March that year, against low-key opposition but achieved little thereafter. At the Italian GP in 1952 there were two factory OSCAs on the grid. When the F1 regulations changed the old F2 OSCAs reappeared, although these were obsolete when the rules changed again in 1954. At the same time, the Orsis decided to go back to racing and in 1954 the Maserati 250F appeared.

The Maseratis found themselves racing against the cars that bore their name... It was short-lived. Both Maserati and OSCA struggled. Maserati withdrew from competition in 1957, while the brothers sold their business to MV Agusta in 1962.

Here today, gone tomorrow

In April 1987 the Lamborghini supercar company was bought by America's Chrysler Corporation, as part of Lee Iacocca's plan to expand Chrysler sales around the world. Iacocca wanted to see Lamborghini in Formula 1, going ahead to head with Ferrari. Former Ferrari team manager Daniele Audetto was hired to run a new company called Lamborghini Engineering to oversee the project and the legendary Mauro Forghieri was appointed technical director to oversee the design and construction of a V12 Formula 1 engine, to be raced under the new 3.5-litre Formula 1 regulations in 1989. A deal was struck in 1988 to supply the new engines to the Larrousse-Calmels team. The 1989 season was not easy but progress was made. Larrousse and Team Lotus used the engines in 1990.

Lamborghini was keen to have its own team, but did not have the budget to do it and so decided to try to find a customer to buy chassis and pay to build up a chassis department. It seemed like a great idea. Towards the end of 1989 an ambitious young Mexican businessman called Fernando Gonzalez Luna announced that he had started a company called Gonzalez Luna Associates, known as GLAS, and was raising money to become the Lamborghini factory team. Forghieri immediately hired designer Mario Tolentino, who had previously worked with Alfa Romeo, EuroBrun and Dallara, and he started work on the chassis that would later become known as the Lambo 291.The car was ready to be launched in June 1990, with Mauro Baldi signed up to test it. On the day before the launch Gonzalez Luna disappeared. To the horror of those in Bologna, it emerged that not only had he disappeared by $20 million has disappeared with him. It was a disaster, although Gonzalez Luna probably thought otherwise as he enjoyed the money in wherever it was that he went to hide.

Lamborghini Engineering tried to find a replacement financier. The obvious choice was Carlo Patrucco, an Italian who had earlier tried to buy Larrousse. He was young and ambitious and had married into the celebrated Cerruti textile family and, as a result, had been put in charge of the Fila clothing company and had become a vice-president of Confindustria, the Italian employers' federation. He then set out to prove that he could make fortunes on his own and was involved in both a print machinery business and in helmet-making companies. He found enough money to get the programme up and running and the newly-named Modena Team signed Nicola Larini and Eric Van de Poele to race in 1991.

At that time there were 34 cars entering each race, but only 30 were allowed to qualify and only 26 raced. There was a brutal one hour of pre-qualifying early each Friday morning, which knocked out four of the cars in pre-qualifying. The problem for Lamborghini was that two of the pre-qualifying teams had very competitive cars: Scuderia Italia and Jordan. The Modena Team made its F1 debut in Phoenix and Larini not only qualified 17th, but raced to seventh. It was a good start. In Brazil, however, the Dallaras and Jordans pre-qualified and so Modena Team was locked out. At the third race, in Imola, Van de Poele qualified 21st and was running fourth in the race, with half a lap to go when his fuel pump failed (or his fuel ran out). After that neither driver pre-qualified again. At the midway point in the season, thanks to Larini's seventh place, the team emerged from pre-qualifying with Brabham, Footwork and AGS being pushed out. The problem was that the level of performance in qualifying improved as a result and with Modena Team struggling for money, Larini qualified only four times and could finish no higher than 16th. It was not enough. The sponsors lost interest, Patrucco, who was in trouble with other businesses as well, could raise no more. The team closed at the end of the year. Lamborghini went back to being just an engine supplier. No-one knows what happened to Gonzalez Luna.

The question beginning with Q

There has never been a Formula 1 constructor with a name beginning with Q. There has been only one F1 driver with a name beginning with Q. Austria's Dieter Quester.

His father Fritz Quester was originally a chimney sweep, but in 1934 he established Quester Baustoffhandel GmbH, distributing building materials. This had developed into Austria's biggest home improvement business, with 24 stores across the country.

Dieter was born in 1939 and grew up in comfortable circumstances after the war. At 18 he was able to afford to begin racing motor boats and he won European outboard 500cc titles in 1958 and 1962. This was followed by a period in motorcycle racing, using BMW, Norton and NSU machinery.

In 1965 he tried cars for the first time and the following year, driving a BMW 1800, was the winner of the Austrian Touring Car Championship. The following year he became a BMW factory driver and married Julianna, the daughter of BMW Motorsport boss Alex Von Falkenhausen.

Quester won European Touring Car titles in 1968 and 1969 in BMW 2002s. He would win again in 1977 in a BMW 3.0 CSL and in 1983 in a BMW 635CSi. He joined the BMW Formula 2 in 1969, alongside Jo Siffert and Hubert Hahne and the following year won the Preis von Baden-Württemberg und Hessen at Hockenheim, beating a class field which included Clay Regazzoni, Ronnie Peterson, Emerson Fittipaldi and Carlos Reutemann. In 1971 he won again, this time at Monza in a March-BMW entered by Eifelland Wohnwagenbau and scored five second places that year and finished third in the European Championship behind Peterson and Reutemann. He was keen to get into F1 but could not get a ride although he eventually made his F1 debut, renting a Surtees for the Austrian GP of 1974. That would be it for F1, but he returned to touring cars and GTs and raced in the BMW Procar series in 1979 and 1980.

He continues to race when he can, despite being in his late seventies.

From the heavens

The 1978 Austrian Grand Prix was Ronnie Peterson's 10th and last victory, a month before he was killed at Monza. It was a wet weekend - on and off - at the Osterreichring, as is often the case in the mountains of Styria.

It had been a summer dominated by the sleek black and gold JPS Lotuses of soon-to-be World Champion Mario Andretti and the popular "Superswede", who had the ground-effect advantage of the superb Lotus 79, which rival teams struggled to understand. Lotus would wrap up the Constructors' Championship in the course of the weekend, with four races still to run.

Peterson was on pole position and won the race while Andretti tangled with Carlos Reutemann's Ferrari on the first lap. The race marked the first podium finish for a rising star by the name of Gilles Villeneuve, who finished third in his Ferrari.

The most unusual aspect of the weekend, however, was that one of the free practice sessions had to be red-flagged for the most eccentric reason in F1 history: a parachute display, which was supposed to have been cancelled because of the low cloud, went ahead as no-one had bothered to tell the parachutists that they were not required. As a result the Formula 1 drivers were faced with the additional hazard of men falling from the sky in a most unpredictable fashion. The session was hurriedly stopped. F1 drivers were less than happy. The parachutists were none too pleased either...

A terrific showdown

The World Championship showdown in 1964 took place in Mexico City on October 25 that year on the Magdalena Mixhuca circuit, now known as the Autódromo Hermanos Rodríguez. There were three British drivers all with a chance of winning the title. Graham Hill in a BRM led the points standings with 39, five ahead of Ferrari's John Surtees with Lotus's Jim Clark with 30 points. At that time Championship points were scored only by the first six cars, with a 9-6-4-3-2-1 system. It was the first time that three constructors went into the last final round of the championship all with a chance of winning the Constructors' title: Ferrari having 43 points, BRM 42 and Lotus 37.

Clark had won three races, but had been winless since the British GP in July, while Surtees and Hill had each won two, as had Brabham's Dan Gurney, although he was not in the running for the title. The other victory had gone to Surtees's Ferrari team-mate Lorenzo Bandini.

Clark took pole position with Gurney alongside and the two went off into the lead with Hill dropping back to 10th because of problems with broken elastic on his goggles. He fought up to third by lap 12 and seemed to be set to win the title until he came under attack from Bandini, who made several attempts to pass the BRM before he made an overly-optimistic lunge on lap 31 and the two cars made contact. Hill spun backwards into the barriers but both cars were able to rejoin, although Hill had a damaged exhaust which meant he was losing power. He made a lengthy pit stop for repairs. His only hope was that Clark would not win the race.

With Hill out of the points, the title was suddenly within Clark's grasp. Surtees had to be second in order to beat him and with Gurney firmly in second, Surtees was in trouble, even if Ferrari ordered Bandini to drop back and let him pass. On lap 64 of 65 Clark's engine failed. Gurney took the lead with Bandini second and Surtees third. Hill was back in a championship winning position with 39 points to Surtees's 38. As the last lap began, Ferrari signalled frantically to Bandini, ordering him to let Surtees overtake. Fortunately, the Italian understood the message and duly allowed Surtees to pass, which meant that he gained two extra points and that gave him 40 points to Hill's 39.

Clark was classified in fifth place, a lap down, but this meant that the Constructors' Championship also went to Ferrari with 45 points to BRM's 42, whereas Lotus would have won it if Clark had won the race.

After the race some suggested that Bandini's move on Hill had been foul play but not even BRM boss Louis Stanley believed the stories. Bandini, Ferrari team manager Eugenio Dragoni and chief engineer Mauro Forghieri all went to visit Stanley after the race to apologise, and Stanley reported that the driver was almost in tears.

It would remain the most exciting World Championship showdown until 1976, but even the amazing finish at Fuji could not beat the finale of 2008 when Lewis Hamilton took the title from Felipe Massa on the very last lap.

A black weekend

There have been some evil weekends in the history of motor racing. At Monza in 1933 three drivers died on the same day; at Imola in 1994 Ayrton Senna and Roland Ratzenberger died and Rubens Barrichello suffered a huge crash, his life being saved by the rapid arrival of Professor Sid Watkins in the medical car.

And then there was Spa in June 1960...

It was a time when British teams were becoming dominant in F1 and that weekend no fewer than eight British drivers were on the 19-car entry list: Graham Hill (31), Innes Ireland and Stirling Moss (both 30), Tony Brooks (28), Alan Stacey (27), and Mike Taylor (26), Jim Clark (24) and Chris Bristow (22).

Things were normal on Friday, but on the hot Saturday afternoon events turned nasty. Moss crashed his Rob Walker Lotus in the latter part of the high-speed Burnenville corner, as the result of a left rear stub axle failure, which resulted in the wheel coming off the car. Moss spun, hit the earth bank on the outside of the corner and was thrown out of the car. The wreck bounced across the road, ending up on the inside of the turn. Stirling suffered two broken legs, three damaged vertebrae and a broken nose. Several drivers stopped to help, but no ambulance appeared and so F1 debutant Taylor set off to drive back to the pits – to get help. On the way his factory Lotus suffered a steering column failure in the high speed La Carrière section. The car went off, ran over ditch and was launched into nearby trees, uprooting the first one it hit. Miraculously, he was not killed, but suffered multiple injuries which would end his racing career.

The next day it was a sombre group who took off at the start of the race. With Moss and Taylor out, the grid was down to only 17 cars, but they ran close together in the early laps. The lap times were very fast, with the fastest lap being set at an average of 136 mph. There were problems for Ireland who spun five times at Blanchimont before going off the road and down a bank, but the chirpy Scottish driver emerged unhurt.

Just after the halfway mark Bristow was involved in a fierce fight with the Ferrari of Willy Mairesse. He was pushing too hard and lost control of his Cooper close to where Moss had crashed the previous day. The car ran up an earth bank and Bristow was decapitated by a barbed wire fence separating the track from an adjoining field. The car then rolled and the driver's body was thrown out on to the track. Clark only narrowly missed running into it.

The race went on. Six laps later Stacey's Lotus went off, just after Burnenville, as he was heading towards the Malmédy section. The car hit the earth bank and then went end over end across the road, flying over the earth bank on the inside of the track through a hedge and ended up down the embankment, where it caught fire. It would emerge later that he had almost certainly been hit in the face by a bird and may have been unconscious even before the car hit the earth bank.

Three of the four youngest British drivers were gone. Only Clark remained.

The bad old days in Europe

For those who think that it will all be so much better when Brexit is done, perhaps one should take a wander back in time and examine the motorsport world before access to Europe was easy and without undue paperwork.

Back in 1956, a 30-year-old Jack Brabham was still struggling to establish himself in Grand Prix racing. He had not started racing until he was 22 and it was seven years after that before he headed to England. He had made his F1 debut the previous year in a Cooper which he had bought from the factory, but he decided that he needed a better car and so sold the Cooper in Australia and used the money to buy a Maserati 250F, which – oddly – had been owned by the Owen Racing Organisation, which manufactured and raced BRMs. The company was working on the new P25, but it was not ready in time for 1955 (in the finest BRM tradition) and so Sir Alfred Owen bought a Maserati in order to have a competitive car for Peter Collins to drive. This also gave his engineers the chance to examine the latest Italian technology…

Collins used the car to win the BRDC International Trophy and the London Trophy and he was then hired by Ferrari.

Owen wanted to get rid of the 250F in early 1956 and Brabham agreed to buy it. Once it was delivered, Jack discovered that the paperwork was not as simple as he had imagined and that, to avoid Purchase Tax, (a sales tax imposed on all items deemed to be "luxury", which was then running at a shocking 60 percent of the price), Owen had only temporarily imported the car and, as a result Brabham could not use the car unless it was exported and then re-imported with different paperwork.

The easiest way to do this was to put the Maserati on a ferry to Guernsey, the

Crown Dependency which, officially, is not part of the United Kingdom. Leaving his Commer transporter in Newhaven, Brabham accompanied the 250F to St Peter Port. It had to be craned on and off the ship because there were no roll-on/roll-off vessels on the route. The ship arrived in the fog and Brabham saw nothing but a wharf, as the car was craned on to the dock and then wheeled across to be loaded on to a different boat, while rubber stamps were applied to paperwork.

They then sailed back to Newhaven where the Maserati slipped in its sling while being unloaded. A terrified Brabham watched in horror, fearing that the car would be dropped on to the dock. Later he wished it had been, because the car brought him nothing but pain. The engine needed to be rebuilt and so it was sent to Italy. Brabham, with his wife Betty and young son Geoffrey, drove to Modena in a Borgward Isabella Combi to pick it up. The rebuild cost a lot more than anticipated and so on the return journey they had to survive on bread and water, because getting money from abroad was complicated and time-consuming. They rushed back to Boulogne, their major fear being that they would run out of petrol before they got there. They just made it and boarded the ferry SS Lord Warden.

They had enough money left for a bowl of soup and had just finished that when the Lord Warden ploughed into a French ship called the Tamba, in fog off Cap Gris Nez. It was a big impact but the Lord Warden was in no danger of sinking and so the ferry continued, with Brabham worried about what he would find when the passengers were allowed back to their vehicles. The result was a Borgward Isabella smashed front and rear, but the Maserati engine undamaged.

Brabham never did race the 250F after that because he never had the money to do so… and instead took a job with John Cooper. This led to back-to-back World Championships in 1959 and 1960, and a third title in 1966 in one of his own cars. In 1979 Jack would be knighted for services to motorsport.

A man of many talents

Alain Prost was 30 when he won his first World Championship, by finishing fourth at Brands Hatch in the European Grand Prix in early October 1985. In the process, he became the first Frenchman to become the FIA Formula 1 World Champion. There were still two races left in the season but Prost could not be caught.

It was announced in France that Alain would be made a Chevalier de la Légion d'Honneur and France celebrated. After the season ended Prost, his pal Jacques Laffite and Jacques's brother-in-law Jean-Pierre Jabouille, all top F1 drivers at the time, were invited to dine with Baron Philippe de Rothschild, the then 83-year-old owner of Bordeaux's celebrated Chateau Mouton-Rothschild in the Medoc.

The chateau had long been considered one of the best in the world and the Baron had campaigned hard in the 1960s to have the chateau declared a Premier Grand Cru: the classification given to only four chateaux, way back in 1855. Rothschild achieved this by making extraordinary wine and by marketing the product in a completely new way, commissioning famous artists to design his labels for him. In addition he played a huge role in popularizing wine around the world by introducing Mouton Cadet, a blend of grapes produced in the Bordeaux region, which was sold at affordable prices. This was a huge success and by the 1980s the company was selling around 17 million bottles a year. Today that has increased to around 25 million, with Mouton Cadet responsible for about half the sales, alongside the Mouton Rothschild and its second and third brands Château Clerc Milon and Château d'Armailhac.

The three drivers and the old baron enjoyed a fine dinner and a bottle of 1881 Chateau Mouton, reckoned to be one of the best vintages ever and they had a great time, telling stories.

You might think that Baron Philippe had little to say to the racing drivers, but he was a man with a life much more colourful than just his wine-making. He was blessed, of course, with money and grew up in the family mansion of the Rue Saint-Honoré, in Paris. This was located between the British Embassy and the Elysées Palace – official residence of the French President. He once described the front door as being sufficiently grand "to admit four giraffes – walking abreast". It was a fairly eccentric childhood, as the family had a troupe of monkeys living with them. One day these escaped and the Rothschilds received a telephone call from the Elysées Palace complaining that the animals were disrupting a rather important cabinet meeting. Just outside Paris, the family also owned the Abbaye les Vaux de Cernay – a 12th century Cistercian abbey which had been transformed into a magnificent country house.

In 1914 Philippe was sent to Chateau Mouton, where his grandmother lived, and fell in love with the place. He soon returned to Paris and enjoyed a playboy lifestyle in the 1920s. He raced yachts in the summer, bobsleighs in the winter and bought the latest cars as they arrived. At 21 he settled in Bordeaux, but raced backwards and forwards to Paris on a regular basis. He had an eye for the ladies and they appreciated the dashing and wealthy young aristocrat. He remained single until he was well over 30.

In 1928 he decided that he would give motor racing a try and entered a Hispano-Suiza in a race from Paris to Nice. He enjoyed the experience and so bought himself a Bugatti Type 37, a 1.5-litre Voiturette version of the Type 35, to race and, using the name "Georges Philippe", he finished second to André Dubonnet (also a wealthy drinks heir) in the Bugatti Grand Prix at Le Mans.

He decided that he would go racing fulltime in 1929 and bought himself a 2.3-litre supercharged Bugatti Type 35C Grand Prix car. He led the GP d'Antibes before crashing and two weeks later finished fourth in the inaugural Monaco GP. Three weeks later he went to Dijon and won the GP de Bourgogne, with his second 35C being driven by Guy Bouriat. Later in the summer he led the German GP at the Nürburgring before damaging the car and being passed by Louis Chiron, but he was invited to join the Bugatti factory team for the Gran Premio de España at San San Sebastián. He finished second, sharing the car with Bouriat. His precocious talent meant that it quickly became rather obvious who he was and his family was not happy. And so "Georges Philippe" disappeared from Grand Prix racing, returning only to race at Le Mans in 1930 in a Stutz Bearcat.

That year he also met the glamorous lady racer Hellé Nice, who had just returned from a promotional tour in the United States. The two became lovers and he not only gave her one of his Grand Prix cars, but also introduced her to Ettore Bugatti. She became a Grand Prix driver in 1931, although by then the couple had gone their separate ways. He went tiger-hunting in 1931 and in 1932 became a movie producer for a while (making one of the early talkies) before marrying a Countess and settling down to a life of wine-making.

When the war came he flew with the French Air Force. He escaped to North Africa but was then sent back to France as a prisoner. He had Jewish roots, of course, and so escaped and went to England to join General de Gaulle's Free French forces, winning the Croix de Guerre in the process.

When he returned to France after the war, he found his old life in ruins. His wife had been deported and murdered, his property had been confiscated and even his French nationality had been revoked. Chateau Mouton had been caught in the middle of a battle between resistants and Germans and the vineyards were damaged and run down. The vignerons had, however, been able to save thousands of bottles of the best vintages by walling up sections of the Mouton chais. Philippe would inherit Mouton when his father died in 1947 and in the 40 years which followed he created a legend – and made a vast fortune.

In his spare time he translated French poetry into English…

Mr Goldenberg, the F1 winner

François Cevert probably shouldn't really have been called Cevert. His father was called Charles Goldenberg. He was a Russian Jew from a well-to-do family, but his father took the family to Paris when Charles was five, believing that it was safer there. He was right. Charles's father was killed in Russia and the money that he sent to support his children outside Russia suddenly stopped arriving. They had to make their own way in the world.

Charles turned to jewellery and he did very well for himself. In 1938 – when Charles was 37 – he met a French woman called Huguette Cevert. They began a relationship, but war came soon afterwards and in 1940 the Germans arrived in Paris. It was not wise to be married to a Jew. Charles went underground, living in a *chambre de bonne* (a servant's room), at the top of the house where Huguette was living. He worked for the Resistance, visiting his wife whenever he could. The couple had four children: Elie, François, Jacqueline and Charles in quick succession. They took their mother's name because legally they had to, as the couple of was not married, and because it was unwise to have a Jewish name in Paris at the time. When the war ended, they lived a more conventional family life in the wealthy suburb of Neuilly-sur-Seine and François soon developed a taste for speed. His first adventures being with his mother's Vespa scooter…

On the road to Portsmouth

Rodney Clarke came from a brainy family. His father was a Professor of Modern History at London University, who married the daughter of another professor. He was sent off to Berkhamsted School in Hertfordshire and from, rather than going to university, decided to apply to for a three-year course in engineering at the Automobile Engineering Training College in Chelsea. At the time this was a hotbed of motor racing activities and Clarke developed an interest in the sport. When he graduated he decided to join the Royal Air Force and became a Flying Officer before being invalided out as a result of serious sinus problems.

At a loose end, he ran a bar, a hotel and then a cinema before deciding to go into the automobile business in 1943. He set up Continental Cars Ltd, his intention being to secure a Bugatti dealership after the war. He bought, sold and serviced cars, while also returning to flying as a ferry pilot. But things didn't quite go to plan… When the war ended the French government seized the factory at Molsheim, on the basis that Bugatti had collaborated with the Germans by selling them his factory. Ettore Bugatti fought the decision but it was not until 1947 that he won the battle. He died a few days later. Thus, there was no Bugatti dealership for Clarke.

Instead he bought, sold and serviced exotic machinery, at one point he was even the owner of one of the celebrated Bugatti Atlantics. In order to expand the business he moved to premises on the main A3 road from London to

Portsmouth, close to the village of Send, near Guildford. He promoted the business by competing in a Bugatti Type 59. It was a busy road in that era, travelled by many wealthy people and so Continental Cars did well.

His customers included two young men, both RAF officers: Mike Oliver, who had flown fighters in the Battle of Britain and in Malta, and Kenneth McAlpine. Oliver joined the business to sell cars, but soon became the head of engine development, while 29-year-old McAlpine, a member of the famous civil engineering family, was impressed by the standard of their engineering and proposed that Clarke build him a sports car. They set up a company called Connaught, a pun using the "conn" from Continental and the "aught" from automobile. Clarke purchased a Lea-Francis 14 Sport, and expensive car when the purchase tax was added and designed a new body, which was built for Connaught by the Leacroft Sheet Metal Works in Egham. The engine was tweaked by Oliver and the car proved to be very promising. No fewer than 14 of them were made as a result. Clarke and Oliver then decided to build a Formula 2 car for the 1951 season. This too was moderately successful and for 1952 Connaught had a factory team – and customer cars.

That year the FIA decided that the World Championship should run to F2 regulations and Connaught suddenly found itself in F1. There was never sufficient money but good engineering meant that the results were solid. When the F1 engine rules changed again in 1954, switching to unsupercharged 2.5-litre engines, Connaught had to find a new engine and turned to Alta, which had a pre-war unit which fitted the requirements. It was developed by Oliver. The Connaught Type B was, however, only ever supposed to be an interim car, while money was found for a ground-breaking rear-engined, monocoque car.

The company achieved little in 1954 and so was more reliant than ever on the largesse of McAlpine, who spent a remarkable £43,000 in the course of the season. The company might have closed that year but for an astonishing win scored at the non-championship Syracuse GP in Sicily by young Tony Brooks in the autumn, beating the factory Maserati factory team. The victory made Brooks became the first British driver to win a continental Grand Prix in a British car since Henry Segrave's triumph at San Sebastián in 1924.

The win convinced Clarke and Oliver to go on, as they suddenly found themselves being offered good start money by race promoters. The bad news was that after the Le Mans disaster in 1955 many races were cancelled. McAlpine also stopped racing, as he married that year.

Despite the efforts of Archie Scott Brown and Stuart Lewis-Evans early in 1957, the axe fell in May that year. Connaught shut down and the assets were auctioned off. Lewis-Evans's manager, a 26-year-old car dealer called Bernie Ecclestone, bought two cars and ran then in 1958 for Lewis-Evans and Roy Salvadori. Ecclestone himself tried to qualify one of the cars at Monaco.

By then, British racing teams were finally breaking through with successes for Vanwall and Cooper. It was the start of a revolution that would create the modern British motorsport industry. Connaught missed the boat...

Clarke went back to the business of selling exotic cars, while Oliver returned to aviation, becoming the test pilot of Folland's Gnat fighter programme and in 1964 the was later a test pilot with Hawker Siddeley before he switched to customer liaison. The two men remained friends until Clarke's death in 1979.

The caravan king

Heinz Hennerici was a character. Born in 1924, he was a Panzer tank commander during World War II and lost his left arm in the course of the fighting. From Mayen, a town in the Eifel region, close to the Nürburgring, he was a keen racing driver – despite having only one arm, and was also the head of the sports department of AC Mayen, the local automobile club.

His twin brother Günther was also into racing, but from 1962 onwards he concentrated on a caravan-building business, Eifelland Wohnwagenbau, which he named after the local region. At the time new technology and the improving economy meant that caravans became very popular, and Hennerici became rich.

Günther Hennerici's dream was to create a German F1 team, the first since Porsche a decade earlier, and he decided to invest all of the Eifelland advertising budget to sponsor motorsport. He started talks with Ford's racing director in Cologne, Mike Kranefuss, to create a German team and Ford agreed to pay for Cosworth engines. The project lacked sufficient time to build a chassis and so it was agreed to buy a March 721, create different bodywork and call it an Eifelland Ford. At the same time, they commissioned Len Terry to design a new car for 1973.

When the first drawings of the planned Eifelland appeared in the German media, industrial designer Lutz Colani, who had adopted the name Luigi, entered the picture, convincing the team that he could do a better job. He had a very high opinion of himself but his futuristic designs were a source of amusement to the F1 regulars. Nonetheless, the Eifelland Ford appeared in South Africa in the hands of Rolf Stommelen.

Hennerici was unable to attend because a fire had wrecked most of his caravan factory and it quickly became clear in the weeks after the fire that he had no money for F1. The team appeared in all the races but it was then announced that

Hennerici had sold the caravan business to Meeth Fensterfabrik GmbH, a window manufacturer, looking to expand into new markets. Meeth had no interest in F1 and cancelled the 1973 plans and simply gave the team to Stommelen, although he ran out of funding after just two races and sold the assets to Brabham's new owner Bernie Ecclestone, who was looking for cheap Cosworth engines. He sold the car to the Hexagon Garage for John Watson to drive.

Mike the Bike

Stanley Michael Bailey Hailwood, otherwise known as "Mike the Bike" was the stuff of legend. He was one of the greatest motorcycle racers in the history of a sport packed with heroes. He went on to become a Formula 1 driver, but never won a race, although perhaps he ought to have done. He took part in 50 Grands Prix between 1963 and 1974, scoring several podiums and being one of the four drivers fighting for the win in the closest ever F1 finish - at Monza in 1971. He was fourth, 0.2secs behind the winner...

Along the way, Mike the Bike not only caused joyous mayhem, often involving enthusiastic young ladies, but also produced a solid series of results in other forms of car racing. He was the European Formula 2 champion of 1972, was on the podium at Le Mans in 1969 in a Ford GT40, shared with David Hobbs, and was a star in Formula 5000.

The stories of Hailwood's adventures have filled many books, but it is often forgotten in the blur of a life lived to the full that Mike the Bike was also awarded the George Medal, Britain's second highest award for civilian gallantry (after the George Cross) for rescuing Clay Regazzoni from a burning BRM during the 1973 South African GP.

It was the third lap of the race and local hero Dave Charlton crashed into Hailwood's Surtees. Most of the cars following managed to avoid the wrecks but Clay Regazzoni arrived in a fight with Jacky Ickx and crashed straight into Hailwood's car. The BRM burst into flames with the Swiss driver unconscious at the wheel. Hailwood's overalls caught fire as he extracted himself from his Surtees, but the flames were extinguished by a fire marshal and then Hailwood went back into the fire to rescue his rival, somehow managing to undo Regazzoni's belts and pull him out of the car to safety. Regazzoni suffered only minor burns as a result...

Ironically, a year later at the Nürburgring, Hailwood's F1 career ended with a violent accident when he lost control of his McLaren after the jump at Pflanzgarten, which left him with a badly broken leg and foot, on a day when

Regazzoni won his first victory with Ferrari. Such is fate.

Mike the Bike would make a sensational return to motorcycle racing in 1978, winning the Isle of Man TT on a Ducati, at the age of 38.

Three years later, having retired from the sport, Hailwood was killed along with his eight-year-old daughter Michelle in a road accident near his home in Warwickshire when his Rover collided with a truck which was performing a dangerous illegal turn on a fast piece of road. They were on their way to pick up some fish and chips.

Three-wheelers in F1

It would be a trick question to ask how many three-wheeled cars have made it on to a Formula 1 podium, but at the same time, it is almost true that this happened.

No F1 car was designed to have three wheels, the Reliant Robin never having had much impact in F1 circles, but drivers have been known to knock wheels off their cars, now and then. Philippe Streiff crossed the finish line at the very first Formula 1 Australian Grand Prix in 1985, on the streets of Adelaide, with all four wheels just about attached, but the front left was not in any regular contact with the road, being dragged along, held on to the car by the remaining suspension links that had not been broken when he collided with his own Ligier-Renault team-mate Jacques Laffite at the hairpin on the penultimate lap.

The race was held in early November and the South Australia city was sweltering in 95-degree F temperatures. This meant that a lot of cars retired but Keke Rosberg, driving a Williams-Honda, somehow managed to get to the chequered flag without overheating, while most of the field disappeared because of the heat. There were engine failures, fires, electrical problems, broken transmissions and overheating brakes and after 81 laps only Rosberg and the two Ligier-Renaults were on the same lap. Laffite, Keke's former Williams team-mate, was being chased by Streiff, with the Tyrrell-Renault of Ivan Capelli, another lap behind, but nonetheless ahead of the delayed Ferrari of Stefan Johansson and an Arrows-BMW driven by Gerhard Berger.

Rosberg was already on his final lap when the two Ligiers collided and, with Capelli taking the chequered flag just behind Rosberg, there was no pressure on Streiff, who limped around the track, hoping that the wheel would stay attached to the car. He made it, to score what would be the best result of his career, although Guy Ligier was unimpressed that Streiff had risked wiping out both cars with his move. In the end, Ligier decided not to offer him a drive for 1986, taking the veteran René Arnoux and leaving Streiff to drive a Tyrrell, thanks to backing from Elf.

In Germany in 1987 Stefan Johansson finished with four wheels, but only three tyres. Does that make it a three-wheeler?

On the way

Formula 1 is a world in which people come and go all the time, either because they were not up to the job, did not want to live the lifestyle or, in the some cases, because they wanted to move on to bigger things. Mike Kranefuss was one of those who passed through F1 on his way to bigger and better things.

Michael Hans August Kranefuss was born German. His family owned a laundry in Münster, in the north of the country, when he arrived in 1938. He was a fan of racing from a very early age, following the exploits of Wolfgang Von Trips in the late 1950s. He worked in the family business but dabbled in racing as well and it was through this that he met a number of German aristocrats, who raced at the time among them Baron Juup Kerckerinck zur Borg, who raced Alfa Romeos and Abarths and Baron Karl Von Wendt. As a result of this he became involved in Von Wendt's campaign to build a racing circuit in the Sauerland in the late 1960s. The region was hilly and heavily-forested with few inhabitants and Von Wendt wanted to build a permanent facility to attract people, and to allow those living in the north of Germany to go racing more easily.

The project failed in 1968 and Wendt left the sport in disgust while Kranefuss was taken on by Jochen Neerpasch, who has also been involved in the project, to work as his assistant at the new Competition Department of Ford Germany. In 1972 Neerpasch went off to BMW and Kranefuss inherited the job and embarked on a programme to develop the Ford Capri in association with Zakspeed.

The Zakspeed Capris would enjoy huge success with drivers such as Dieter Glemser, Jochen Mass, Klaus Ludwig and Hans Heyer. Glemser, Mass and Heyer all became European Touring Car Champions in the cars in 1971, 1972 and 1974 and Glemser won the 1971 Spa 24 Hours with Alex Soler-Roig and the following year Mass won with Hans Stuck.

The success led to Kranefuss becoming head of competition for the whole of Europe at the age of 37. While Ford continued to do well in touring cars, he increased the company's involvement in rallying and in 1979 Bjorn Waldegard won the World Rally Champion in 1979 with the Ford Escort RS. The following year Kranefuss was called to Ford headquarters in Detroit and appointed head of the new Ford Special Vehicle Operations, in control of all of Ford's global sporting programmes.

Ford's activities grew in TransAm and in NASCAR, with Bill Elliott winning the Winston Cup in 1988 and Alan Kulwicki in 1992. There was success in CART in 1992 and 1993, with Nigel Mansell winning the title in the latter season, and in Formula 1, Kranefuss supported Benetton with Nelson Piquet, Sandro Nannini, Roberto Moreno and ultimately Michael Schumacher

He quit Ford in 1993 and tried to establish his own Indycar team, but that did not work out and so he went into business with Carl Haas in NASCAR, the team running its first full season in 1995 with John Andretti. The team did not win a race and late in 1997 Haas sold his shares to Roger Penske and the Penske-Kranefuss Racing enjoyed rather more success with driver Jeremy Mayfield, who won three races between 1998 and 2000. At the end of 2000 Kranefuss sold his shares to Penske and retired with plenty of money in the bank. Two years later he tried to start Falcon Cars to build cars for the Indy Racing League, but that never really got off the ground. By then he was 64 and he disappeared to a quiet retirement in Mooresville, North Carolina.

Sir Nobuhiko

It would be incorrect to refer to Nobuhiko Kawamoto as Sir Nobuhiko, because as a Japanese citizen he does not have the right to use the title Sir – despite the fact that he is a Knight Commander of the Most Excellent Order of the British Empire – and is allowed to put the letters KBE after his name.

Kawamoto was born in Tokyo, early in 1936. One of his first memories was watching Japanese warplanes taking off for a bombing raids in China. He became fascinated by machines. The war ended with Japan's defeat when Kawamoto was nine, and his teenage years were spent with Japan occupied by U.S. forces. As Japan recovered, he studied engineering at Tōhoku University in Sendai and, while there, he won a scholarship, using the money to race a second-hand motorcycle, while his family continued to send him funds for tuition and to live. Later, when he had a good job, he repaid his father. At the same time, he was the leader of a club which was founded to rebuild the cars the Americans had left behind when they departed in 1952.

After completing his Masters, he joined Honda's research and development division in 1963, having become a big fan of the company when Soichiro Honda decided to take on the world in motorcycle racing, trying to win the Isle of Man TT. Kawamoto was soon sent to Europe as a designer and development engineer for the Honda F1 programme, writing long technical reports about each race and mailing them home to Japan. The team learned quickly and started to winning, but withdrew from the sport in 1968 after Jo Schlesser was killed driving one of the Honda F1 cars at Rouen.

Kawamoto moved over to production vehicles in Japan, working on the design of the Civic, which appeared in 1972, and the advanced CVCC engine. He became head of Honda R&D in 1981. This led to the company returning to racing with a successful Formula 2 engine programme with Ralt, which resulted in three European F2 titles between 1982 and 1984. In 1983 the Honda board decided to return to F1 as an engine supplier and over the next nine seasons won a string of F1 titles with Williams and then McLaren, the company enjoying unprecedented success. The Honda tradition had always been have to racers at the head of the firm: Soichiro Honda was followed in 1973 by Kiyoshi Kawashima, who had led the Isle of Man TT team. When he retired in 1983, Tadashi Kume, who had designed engines for the TT and F1 programmes, took over. And in 1990 Kawamoto became the fourth president of Honda.

The company was then facing a hostile takeover by Mitsubishi, had an ageing product range and was not paying enough attention to what the market wanted. Unpalatable though it was to him, Kawamoto ended Honda's F1 programme in 1992. In the years that followed he focussed the company on its technology and products and turned the business around, restructuring and increasing profits from $540 million in 1990 to $1.78 billion six years later.

Kawamoto the racer remained. He quietly oversaw the development of a Honda-Honda F1 test car in Japan. He even drove it. He was keen to have Honda back in F1 and in 1998 moves began to have a Honda team, with a prototype designed by Harvey Postlethwaite and built by Dallara, but Kawamoto was then pushed out by other factions at Honda and the project died. Honda engines would return to F1 with BAR in 2000 and the firm would later take over the team and run a factory programme from 2006 to 2008, but without Kawamoto, the ethos – and the level of success – were different.

The Captain

Early in 2017 Roger Penske turned 80. He is an extraordinary businessman. Starting out with a single car lot in Pennsylvania, Penske has built an amazing empire, including the publicly-traded Penske Automotive Group, one of the world's biggest car dealers, a truck rental and leasing business and transportation logistics firms. Today he is reckoned to be worth about $1.5 billion and his empire employs around 47,000 people, with annual revenues of tens of billions. He has sat on many corporate boards, including General Electric, the Home Depot and Delphi Automotive. He has invested huge amounts in trying to revive the city of Detroit, including being the chairman of Super Bowl XL.

But Penske is a racer at heart and each weekend his racing teams are in action in IndyCar and NASCAR. Penske Racing has won the Indy 500 no fewer than 16 times between 1972 and 2017, in addition to winning 14 IndyCar titles, including a dominant season in 2016. The team won the Daytona 500 in 2008 with Ryan Newman and added a second win in 2015 with Joey Logano. In 2010 Brad Keselowski took Penske to the title in the NASCAR Xfinity Series and two years later won the Sprint Cup.

What few people remember is that Roger Penske was not only a Formula 1 team owner – with a team that won a race, but he was also an F1 driver as well.

Penske was always mad about cars and went to see his first Indianapolis 500 with his dad in 1951. He was 14. Born in Shaker Heights, Ohio – a nice part of Cleveland – he started out riding motorcycles. After smashing himself up at 16 he started working in a gas station, buying, rebuilding and selling sports cars, beginning with an MG. He raced the cars when he could, did hillclimbs and then some midget races at Sportsman Park, Cleveland, before heading off to study business administration at Lehigh University in Bethlehem, Pennsylvania. He started racing a Chevrolet in SCCA events, went to a racing school at the Marlboro Speedway near Washington and then dropped out of school and become an aluminium salesman for Alcoa. He got married, settled down and quit racing – and then went back to it again.

He won his first national title with the SCCA in 1961 and that year raced a customer Cooper-Climax in the United States Grand Prix at Watkins Glen, finishing eighth. The following year he won the USAC road racing championship and driving a Zerex Special won the Riverside, Monterey and Puerto Rico GPs, the Nassau TT and his class in the Sebring 12 Hours. He competed in the US GP a second time, driving a Lotus-Climax to ninth place.

In 1963 he tried his hand at NASCAR, won the Riverside 250 and led the Yankee 300 before deciding that it was time to retire and concentrate on business. He was 27. He quit Alcoa and took a job with McKean Chevrolet in Philadelphia. A year later he bought his first dealership and started to acquire more and more of them. He was soon making enough to start Penske Racing in 1966, in league with engineer-driver Mark Donohue. The team won its first CanAm race at Mosport Park with a Lola that year and in 1967 Donohue won the US Road Racing Championship and in 1968 dominated TransAm in a Penske Camaro.

The success just kept coming with title after title and victory in the Daytona 24

Hours, not to mention to Rookie of the Year at Indianapolis, finishing seventh in the team's first visit. Success followed success and the team's high point was in 1972 when Donohue won the Indianapolis 500 and the team won the CanAm title with George Follmer driving a Porsche 917.

Further successes were added in NASCAR and at the end of 1974 Penske decided to enter a team in Formula 1. Penske the salesman talked the First National City bank into sponsoring the operation and a factory was opened in Poole, Dorset. The first car – the Penske PC1 – appeared at the Canadian Grand Prix in 1974 where Donohue finished 12th. In 1975 the team switched to a March chassis but then in Austria Donohue suffered a tyre failure and crashed in the warm-up. It seemed that he was not badly hurt, but he died three days later from brain injuries.

Penske decided to go on and ran John Watson later in the year. The following season Wattie drove a new PC4 to victory in Austria, a year after Donohue's death. But Penske realised that F1 was not really sustainable for his team and sold the operation at the end of 1976. The factory in Poole began building Indycars. The PC5 appeared in the summer of 1977 and Tom Sneva used one of the cars to win the USAC title in 1977 and followed up with a second championship in the PC6 in 1978. In 1979 Rick Mears gave Penske its third consecutive title... and it went from there.

Occupation: Gentleman

These days Johnnie Walker is the Official Whisky of Formula One, hoping to use the sport to increase its sales around the world. You can often see Johnnie Walker signage around the tracks.

The brand is owned by Diageo plc, the world's largest producer of spirits. Johnnie Walker was a partner of McLaren from 2005 until 2016, but in 2017 moved to Force India, replacing Smirnoff - the vodka brand being another Diageo product.

But Johnnie Walker's links with actually F1 go back 100 years - to the day Robert Ramsay Campbell Walker was born.

Rob Walker was the great-grandson of Johnnie Walker, the Scottish grocer who began selling his own brand of blended whisky in the family shop. It was Johnnie Walker's son Alexander who really built the business, expanding production and marketing the whisky all over the British Empire. Alexander had a string of children, the oldest being John Walker (born in 1863 and named after Alexander's father). John moved to Australia in his twenties, married a local girl called Colina Campbell and in 1889 they had a son they called James. Seven years later, at the age of 33, John Walker died suddenly. His widow died in 1905, when James was 16 and he decided to move to England. He settled in Farnham, married and had two sons, John (in 1914) and Rob (in 1917). Early in 1921 James died at the age of 32, leaving his wife with two small boys, aged six and three. He left a fortune of £300,000 in his will in addition to impressive annual revenues.

When Rob was seven and on holiday in France, he was taken to watch the Grand Prix de Boulogne, a combined voiturette and cyclecar race. He was sitting next to the wife of Bunny Marshall, the driver who won the race in a Brescia Bugatti, who explained to him everything that was happening. He became an instant racing fanatic. Two years later, in 1926, his mother married a man nearly twice her age. Rob's step-father, Sir Francis Lacey, was secretary of Marylebone Cricket Club - and the first person ever to be knighted for services to sport. Three years later Lady Lacey bought a large estate in Wiltshire. Rob was sent off to school and soon had a Morgan sports car hidden away in a local garage. His mother was so alarmed that she offered to buy him any non-racing car he wanted. He chose a Rolls Royce.

As soon as he was old enough, however, he went racing, starting out with a Lea-Francis at the Lewes Speed Trial. He then bought an ex-Prince Bira Delahaye which he raced at Brooklands and at Le Mans, finishing eighth overall with Ian Connell. He had already been banned from flying by this point, having run into trouble by buzzing a local horse race. However, when the war came, Britain needed all the pilots it could find and Robert joined the Fleet Air Arm as a pilot. In 1940 he married Betty Duncan and agreed to stop racing, if he would be allowed to take part in hillclimbs and speed trials once the war was over. He was posted to Malta and survived his ship being torpedoed en route. He would later be grounded because of poor night vision.

As soon as he was demobbed, he went back to racing, winning a series of minor events before establishing the Pippbrook Garage in Dorking, initially preparing sports cars for Tony Rolt before being convinced by Rolt to buy a 1927 Delage that had been revamped for Dick Seaman in the 1930s by Giulio Ramponi. This was still very competitive, although Walker would later fit an ERA engine to give it more horsepower. He moved on to buying Connaughts and entered Formula 1 as a private team in 1957. The team would operate for the next 11 seasons and would win a total of nine Grands Prix, mainly with Stirling Moss, notably an historic victory in Argentina in a Cooper in 1958, the first victory for a rear-engined F1 car. Two years later at Monaco, Moss became the first man to win a Grand Prix in a Lotus.

Rob tried to build his own Walker F2 car but this was not a great success and so he remained a privateer, buying the equipment he required. Among the projects, Walker helped to develop the four-wheel-drive Ferguson F1 car, which

Rolt had built. In April 1962 Moss was seriously injured racing for another team at Goodwood and Walker hired Maurice Trintignant but there would be tragedy for the team at the end of the year when he rented a car to Ricardo Rodriguez in Mexico and the youngster was killed. Six weeks later Gary Hocking crashed one of Walker's cars in South Africa and also died. Walker would go on running F1 cars until 1968, giving Jochen Rindt his F1 debut and running Jo Bonnier and Jo Siffert. Graham Hill joined him for a while, which enabled Walker to sign a sponsorship deal with Brooke Bond Oxo, but when Hill departed he decided to take the money to Surtees to run Mike Hailwood. When Hailwood retired in1974, Walker decided it was a good moment to stop and he began working instead as an F1 journalist with the US magazine *Road & Track*. The team was briefly revived in 1975 to run Alan Jones in a Hesketh but after that Walker remained a chronicler of F1 until the 1990s, when his advancing years made travel increasingly difficult.

Walker is still the only private team owner to win Formula 1 World Championship races.

A strange lot

Formula 1 press officers are the most diverse group in the sport. Today, there is specialised training and languages are important, but PR in F1 has always been a job with no set qualifications. And a look back reveals that while some PRs were ex-journalists (as might be expected), others had amazing backgrounds.

Anna Guerrier, a former McLaren PR, for example, was a theatrical, trained at Guildford School of Music and Drama. She ended up on the radio before joining McLaren. Ben Taylor, a one-time Tyrrell PR man, had previously promoted English sausages and pork pies for the Meat and Livestock Commission. Peugeot's Jean-Claude Lefèbvre was a racing driver and rallycross champion while Chris Williams and Dany Hindenoch (both Ligier PR men) were rally co-drivers, although the latter also ran his own agency for fashion models. There was also the extraordinary Christine Gorham (Arrows), who arrived in F1 with sponsor MTV. Born in Austria, she had worked with most of the big name rock and roll stars – and was even married to one.

Mercedes's Wolfgang Schattling, on the other hand, started out as a school teacher, while university lecturer Stuart Sykes (Stewart GP) and Ellen Bernfeld (Tyrrell), formerly of the Oriental Antiquities Department of the British Museum, were notable additions to this diverse world, as was Phillip Morris's Nigel Wollheim, who started out with Pirelli, because he spoke four languages fluently. He had previously been a manufacturer of snow boots.

There was the Italian aristocrat Francesco Longanesi Cattani, the son of a celebrated submarine captain, who came to F1 with the FIA after a career as a professional yachtsman, before becoming *aide-de-camp* to Prince Rainier of Monaco. Other PRs, notably Sauber's Gustav Busing and Marlboro's Agnès Carlier, came from the world of politics, while sports also provided some interesting characters, such as Texaco's Paul Bray, a former handball international, and Brazil's Betise Assumpção, a former volleyball player, who would become Ayrton Senna's PR.

There were some interesting transfers within PR as well, with Sabine Marcon, a Ford PR, having been EuroDisney's first international ambassador, and Benetton's Elizabeth Wright, who arrived in F1 from Vogue magazine in New York.

Of the current generation, McLaren's Silvia Hoffer was trained as an architect at the elite Politecnico in Milan, before designing merchandise for Bugatti and then getting her first PR role with Ducati. Toro Rosso's Fabiana Valenti is also remarkable. She was previously a postwoman, who represented Italy in archery...

ATS or ATS?

There have been two F1 teams called ATS. The first was an Italian organization, known as Automobili Turismo e Sport; the second a German outfit known as Auto Technisches Spezialzübehor. Bizarrely, the first was the second of two F1 teams run by its owner, while the second was the first of two F1 teams run by its proprietor.

The original ATS was owned by Giovanni Volpi, the second Count of Misurata, who inherited a great deal of money at the age of 21 and set up a racing team, which entered F1 in 1961 as Scuderia Serenissima. The Count soon fell out with his partners and so joined forces with a group of disaffected Ferrari employees, including chief designer Carlo Chiti and team manager Romolo Tavoni, to form ATS in 1962. Later, after this had failed, Volpi built the Serenissima V8 engine that was used (briefly) by McLaren.

The second ATS was launched by German aluminium wheel magnates Günther Schmid and Erich Stahlschmidt, in order to publicise their business. They bought Roger Penske's F1 cars at the end of 1976 and a year later also acquired the assets of the March F1 team. Neither programme was successful so Schmid began building his own ATS cars in 1979. In the end the two partners fell out over money and in 1985 ATS dropped out of F1. Schmid sold his shares in the wheel business and bought a rival firm called RIAL Leichtmetallfelgen GmbH. He returned to F1 in 1988 with a new team called Rial. It closed after just two years.

There have also been two F1 drivers called G. Berger, but that is another story.

A very cool sponsor

British American Tobacco (BAT) is well known for having been a motor racing sponsor. The cigarette firm bought the Tyrrell team at the end of 1997 as the company's then CEO Martin Broughton was keen to use F1 to promote the sales of Lucky Strike, which it had acquired in 1993 from American Tobacco, and the 555 brand, which BAT was keen to grow in Asia. The purchase of Tyrrell was basically to acquire its entry and a completely new team was put together in Brackley by Craig Pollock and Adrian Reynard. The team raced as Tyrrell in 1998 but was then launched as BAR in 1999, with a bizarre two-sided colour scheme with Lucky Strike on one side of the car and 555 on the other. This was the result of the team ignoring the rulebook and trying to run its cars in two different liveries.

The team continued under BAT ownership until the end of 2005 when it was sold to Honda, BAT by then having come under new leadership. The team would later transform into Brawn GP and more recently in to Mercedes AMG Petronas.

But this was not the first time that BAT had been in F1. In the 1980s it had funded several teams, trying to promote the European sales of its low-tar Barclay brand, which was manufactured by its US subsidiary Brown & Williamson. The sponsorship was largely related to Belgian driver Thierry Boutsen and sponsored him at Arrows in 1984, 1985 and 1986. Boutsen then moved to Benetton and the sponsorship went to Williams, but the two were back together in 1989 and 1990 when Thierry joined Williams. The sponsorship moved on to Jordan in 1992 and 1993 and Boutsen turned up there too.

But even this was not BAT's first foray into Formula 1 because back in the early 1970s, the company was a big F1 sponsor - but not with a tobacco brand.

Sponsorship was just beginning in Formula 1 at the time and Imperial Tobacco, which owned some of BAT's shares, had started the ball rolling in 1968 by supporting Team Lotus with its Gold Leaf brand. This would be switched to the black and gold of John Player Special in 1972. BAT was in the process of diversifying into non-tobacco businesses at the time, as a result of the new chairman Denzil Clarke believing that this was a good strategy. In 1967 BAT had acquired the venerable cosmetic, fragrance and toiletry company Yardley of Bond Street. It was the Swinging Sixties and under BAT ownership Yardley associated itself with the rising fashion stars of the era - notably Jean Shrimpton and Twiggy - and embraced the cultural revolution that was taking place.

Yardley was cool and, after Clarke handed over BAT to a new chairman, Richard Dobson, in 1970, he decided that motor racing was also cool and agreed a two-year deal for Yardley to sponsor BRM, for the princely sum of £50,000. The drivers were Pedro Rodrigez, Jo Siffert and Howden Ganley in white BRMs, featuring black, brown and gold Yardley logos. It was a difficult time in F1 history and the Yardley BRM team suffered. Rodriguez was killed in a sports car race at the Norisring in July, but the team won in Austria (thanks to Siffert) and at Monza (thanks to Peter Gethin) and by the end of the year was running four cars with Gethin and Helmut Marko (now of Red Bull fame) alongside Siffert and Ganley. The season would end in tragedy, however, when Siffert crashed and died in a fire at the season-ending Victory Race at Brands Hatch. BRM boss Louis Stanley went Fribourg to attend Siffert's funeral and then, having heard that Philip Morris wanted to get into F1, drove to Marlboro headquarters in Lausanne to present a sponsorship proposal to Ronnie Thomson, the President of Philip Morris Europe. A two-year £100,000 contract was signed a few days later.

Yardley seems to have been happy to see the back of BRM and agreed a new deal with McLaren, supporting Denny Hulme and Peter Revson (and his replacement in several events Brian Redman). The team expanded to a third car for Jody Scheckter for the US Grand Prix. Hulme won the South African GP and the non-championship Gold Cup at Oulton Park, but otherwise the team was winless. The sponsorship continued in 1973 with Hulme, Revson and Scheckter on occasion. Revson won twice, in Britain and Canada, while Hulme took victory in Sweden.

By the end of the season, however, McLaren was keen to sign with Marlboro, which had had enough of BRM by then. McLaren and Brabham were battling for the sponsorship, which would include Texaco sponsorship and Emerson Fittipaldi. Yardley threatened McLaren with legal action but the enterprising Teddy Mayer managed to find a solution with the team being split with two Marlboro cars for Fittipaldi and Hulme and a third car, run by McLaren's joint managing director, Phil Kerr, for Mike Hailwood, in Yardley colours. Fittipaldi would win the title in 1974 while Hailwood's season ended with a broken leg. He was replaced for two races by David Hobbs and then by Jochen Mass.

At the end of the year Yardley pulled out of F1.

Light on his feet

Raymond Mays was an accomplished and respected racing driver in the 1930s. He founded English Racing Automobiles (ERA) and later British Racing Motors (BRM) and would eventually be appointed a Commander of the Order of the British Empire for his services to the sport.

What is less known is that the former Grenadier Guards officer was just mad about the theatre. As a young man, he was besotted by an actress called José Collins, who was the star of the musical "The Maid of the Mountains" which ran for three years at Daly's Theatre, near Leicester Square. He saw the show no fewer than 84 times. Mays was also a keen dancer and among his motor racing trophies was a cup he won for winning a dancing competition at the Casino Ballroom in Skegness, partnered by his cousin, Nona Agnew.

He was also a member of the Bourne Amateur Operatic Society in Lincolnshire, where he lived, and appeared in a production of *The Quaker Girl* at the Bourne Corn Exchange in 1930.

Grand Prix People

In 1990 the Canadian F1 writer Gerald Donaldson was commissioned to write a book called "Grand Prix People", telling the stories of more than 100 people working in the Formula 1 world at the time. "It was a fascinating assignment," Donaldson said. "Whenever I switched on my tape recorder I was prepared to be enthralled. I was never disappointed. But I was constantly surprised."

The book concludes with Bernie Ecclestone's assessment of Grand Prix People. "They're all a bit mad!" he said. "That's all…" The more people you meet in Formula 1, the more you appreciate that they are very often special people, folk with many and varied talents and motivation to get things done and to take risks that others would not take to get what they want. Life is for living. It's a gamble…

That was, quite literally, the case with Fred Gamble, a member of the Formula 1 fraternity back in the 1960s. Fred was an American, and there were not many of them in F1 in those days. He had been a Grand Prix driver himself, which was quite an achievement in itself. Ultimately he left a mark, having set up Goodyear's racing operations in Europe, which led to a remarkable 368 F1 victories in 494 starts, providing tyres for 24 World Champions and 26 Constructors' titles. For some of that time Goodyear was a sole supplier, but the statistics show that this was no more so than Pirelli or Bridgestone, who each had their own periods of monopoly but are still nowhere near Goodyear's total.

Gamble was the son of an architect, who had a Masters from the Massachusetts Institute of Technology and lectured at the University of Michigan. Fred was born in Pittsburgh, Pennsylvania, but the family soon decided to try something new and headed south to Florida where they settled in Fort Lauderdale and Harry Gamble went to work with the celebrated Miami architect Russell Pancoast. It was a good time to be an architect in Florida, with the Art Deco district in Miami developing and the city beginning to recover from the Great Depression. More and people more people had money and that meant more and more people had automobiles. The young Fred Gamble was fascinated by them.

Sadly, his father died in 1947, when Fred was only 15 and at high school. The teenager began to get involved in illegal street races in 1930s machinery and also helped a family friend run occasional races on the runways of an old naval base at nearby Davie. He then join the US Army Air Force in order to qualify for a university education, under the terms of the GI Bill. He served two tours in Korea, working as a radio operator during the Korean War. In his last year of service he was posted to Castle Air Force base in Merced, California, where he got into the booming local sports car scene for a while before returning to Florida to attend the University of Florida in Gainesville, studying at the School of Journalism and Communications, while at the same time running the university sports car club.

In 1958 he acquired a disassembled Crosley Hot Shot, which he rebuilt as a special called the Gambini MK1, which he raced that summer. After graduation he took a job as the assistant advertising manager of Jarrard Motors in Pensacola, a dealership which imported European sports cars and ran a team of Triumphs in local SCCA events. Gamble also started writing for various motorsport publications. This allowed him to fund some races with an MGA and, at a race meeting in Miami, he ran into Lloyd Casner, a PanAm pilot who was known to the Racing world as "Lucky".

Casner was planning to take a team to Europe and Gamble volunteered to join without pay, aiming to make a living as a journalist going to the European races. The Casner Motor Racing Division (Camoradi) was indeed lucky. Casner's project came just as Goodyear decided to get into racing and in January 1959 the company agreed to provide Camoradi with substantial financial support and all the tyres it needed. Chevrolet, which was not supposed to compete because of an agreement between the manufacturers not to go racing, provided two Corvettes and covert support, while other big name companies joined the operation as associate supporters when they heard that Goodyear was involved. The team headed to Europe in September 1959 and quickly went into action, buying a birdcage Maserati sports car from the ailing Italian company and two Porsches from the estate of Jean Behra: a lightweight Carrera sports car and the Behra-Porsche Formula 2 car. Camoradi USA became, in effect, the Maserati works team that summer as the factory could not afford to race and the so the well- funded US team attracted a string of star drivers in the summer of 1960, with Gamble racing when the opportunities arose.

Casner was often back in Miami, so Gamble effectively ran the European operation, living in Modena, Italy. That summer Fred landed an entry for the Behra-Porsche in the German Grand Prix, but Porsche's racing boss Huschke von Hanstein vetoed the plan because the car still had a factory engine fitted. In September, however, another opportunity arose when the British F1 teams decided to boycott the Grand Prix of Europe at Monza after the Italians decided to run the event on the high banking. This opened the way for Formula 2 cars to join the entry and Gamble jumped at the chance, firstly because he wanted to be an F1 driver and secondly because of the not inconsiderable starting money on offer. He raced the Camoradi Behra Porsche. He qualified 14th out of 16 and finished 10th and last. But he was a Grand Prix driver…

Finding Casner's business methods rather dubious, Gamble decided to quit Camoradi and returned to the US that autumn, where he found a job in the advertising department of Standard-Triumph North America. He moved on from there to join Carroll Shelby, selling Cobras in California where he soon met Goodyear's Director of Racing, Tony Webner. The latter was looking for an assistant to set up operations for Goodyear in Europe and, hearing about his experiences with Camoradi, asked Gamble if he was interested.

And so in 1964 Fred headed off to unglamorous Wolverhampton to set up Goodyear's motorsport operations in Europe. The result was a string of success for the Akron tyre-maker with three Le Mans victories in 1965, 1966 and 1967 and Goodyear's first F1 victory with Richie Ginther's Honda in Mexico in 1965. In 1966 the company won four races and took the World Championship with Jack Brabham. The success was repeated in 1967 with Denny Hulme.

In 1968 Gamble decided to move back to the US to switch into a more senior role in Goodyear's sales division, handing the motorsport job over to a young Leo Mehl, who would be the dominant name in Goodyear's racing until his retirement in 1996.

After retiring from Goodyear, Gamble went on to promote a ski resort in Snowmass, just outside Aspen in Colorado, before retiring to Hawaii, where he kept fit with regular surfing, even in his seventies.

A fairytale to finish...

History can be a magical thing. People and places have their day in the sun and then fade away, leaving few traces of what once they were. One can find magnificent follies in tiny villages and wonder how and why such a thing could exist. History ebbs and flows. Empires rise and fall, some lost forever in the mists of time. Where was Eldorado? Did Atlantis really exist? Were these places real or did the storytellers, sitting around fires on cold dark nights, weave magical words together to create magnificent places that lived only in the imaginations of the listeners? Who was King Arthur and where was Camelot? Stories were passed down through the generations to become folklore and fairytales.

In the late Seventeenth Century, a French aristocrat called Charles Perrault dedicated himself to collecting and writing down these stories and put Little Red Riding Hood, Cinderella, Puss in Boots and Sleeping Beauty into books 100 years before the Brothers Grimm told their tales and long before Hans Christian Andersen wrote his celebrated stories.

Perrault lived in the Château de Viry, in the countryside to the south of Paris. It was built on a hillside overlooking the lowlands where the mighty Seine was met by the lively Orge. Through these meadows ran the main road south from Paris's Porte d'Italie en route to faraway Italy. A century later the Emperor Napoleon would classify the road as Route Nationale 7, and in time it became the road that Tout Paris drove, on their way to the Côte d'Azur.

The chateau sat in the village of Viry-sur-Orge, which was next to a settlement called Châtillon-sur-Seine, the incongruous names resulting from the confluence of the two rivers. After the French Revolution, during a surge of frenzied efficiency, the two villages were tied together with red tape to create the Viry-Châtillon commune.

The chateau is gone now and today there is a busy boulevard called the Avenue Marmont, which runs across the site, rising up to a drab industrial roundabout, ringed by fast food restaurants and a sizeable shopping centre. This is the Rond-Point Amédée Gordini, named in honour of the Italian engine wizard who kept French motorsport alive in the 1950s, in the era before Elf came along and sparked a new golden age.

Today, the name Viry-Châtillon is known the world over for the Renault facility, where the magicians who followed Gordini designed and developed the company's Formula 1 engines.

The factory that Gordini built in 1968 overlooks the roundabout, while the A6 motorway (which never sleeps) is alongside. The Renault facility is on a piece of land that Gordini found thanks to his friendship with the local mayor Henri Longuet, who had won the European speedboat title in 1956. Longuet wanted Viry-Châtillon to be a sporting centre and funded the construction of football fields, tennis courts, an ice rink, a swimming pool and a nautical centre, not to mention a ski chalet in Megève, in the Alps, where the children of Viry-Châtillon could go to learn to ski. Having the celebrated Gordini racing company in his commune was just what Longuet wanted.

What is not well known in the racing world is that before Gordini, Viry-Châtillon was famous for things other than Perrault. Go a few blocks to the north of the factory, on the flat land that lay below the old chateau, and you will find clues: the Boulevard Guynemer, and streets named after Nungesser et Coli, Roland Garros, Védrines and Eugène Lefebvre. You don't need to be much of an expert to recognise that these were all early aviators. The reason for this is that Viry-Châtillon was the site of the world's very first properly-organised aerodrome, opened amid much excitement in May 1909 when Léon Delagrange flew five times around the circular landing field at about 20 feet, watched by tens of thousands of fascinated people. The aerodrome was named Port-Aviation and had hangars and workshops for the aviators. A couple months after it opened an unknown flyer called Louis Blériot flew 24 laps circuits around the field, preparing to fly across the English Channel, a feat that made him a household name. Shortly afterwards Lefebvre wrote his name into the history books by becoming the first person to die while piloting a powered aeroplane. A matter of days after that, the Count Charles de Lambert, the first person in France to be taught to fly by Wilbur Wright, took off from Port-Aviation and overflew Paris, astonishing tens of thousands as he flew past the Eiffel Tower. And so it went on: three years later Port-Aviation was where the dashing Adolphe Pégoud became the first man to fly an aircraft upside-down and followed up by being the first to loop the loop.

During the First World War, Port-Aviation became a military base, housing a flying school which trained nearly 600 French pilots before being handed over to the Belgian Air Force to provide a flying school for their exiled pilots.

The problem was that as the horsepower of the aero-engines increased, so the hills around Port-Aviation became more and more of a drawback. And so the development of engines ultimately destroyed the fame of Viry-Châtillon… the aerodrome was abandoned after the war, the hangars and workshops were demolished.

Half a century later, history worked its magic and engine development put Viry-Châtillon back on the world map, a fairytale that even Perrault himself would have appreciated…

A

Abarth, Carlo 45, 51, 94, 133
Abbaye les Vaux de Cernay 126
Abidjan-Nice raid 95
Abu Dhabi GP 7
Académie Française 11
Acat, Raymond 60
Adelaide F1 circuit 18
Admiralty Research Laboratory 88
Aérodrome de la Champagne 34
AFM 7, 97, 99
Agache, Alfred 77
Agadir GP 80
Agnelli, Giovanni 48
Agnew, Nona 143
AGS F1 13, 95, 119
Ain-Diab circuit 80
Aintree circuit 114
Akron, Ohio 145
Albers, Christijan 13
Albert Park circuit 70
Albi circuit 81, 103
Alborghetti, Mario 86
Alcoa 111
Alesi, Jean 18, 63, 64
Alexander Engineering 112
Alfa Romeo 35, 38, 43, 45, 46, 48, 63, 64, 65, 71, 85, 106, 114, 119
Allanet, Pierre 60
Allard Motor Company 74
Allison, Cliff 39
Allison, James 39
Alonso, Fernando 18
Alpine F1 car (A500) 106
Alta Car & Engineering Co 33, 90
American Grand Prize 73
American Tobacco 141
Amon, Chris 18, 44, 61, 70
Anakata Wind Energy 100
Anchor Motor Company 112
Anderson, Gary 84, 85
Anderstorp circuit 75
André, Charles 105
André, Delphine 105
Andretti, John 134
Andretti, Mario 19, 20, 45, 53, 55, 121
Andrews, Keith 47
Anfa circuit 103
Ansaldo car company 67
Anson Cars 84
Antibes GP 127
Antwerp 33, 71
Apicella, Marco 13
Arcangeli, Luigi 118
Ardmore 109
Argentine GP 40, 110, 138
Arnoux, René 64, 107, 133
Arrows F1 team 101, 132
Arundell, Peter 22, 30
Arzani, Egidio 87
Åsberg, Sven 75
Ascari, Alberto 19, 47
Ascari, Antonio 48
Ashcroft, Peter 30

Association Internationale des Automobiles Clubs Reconnus (AIACR) 10, 62
Assumpção, Betise 140
Aston Martin 35, 36, 102, 114
Audetto, Daniele 119
Audi AG 99
Auriol, Hubert 83
Aurora F1 series 53
Austin Healey 58
Austin, Herbert 70
Austin, Irene 70
Austin Rover Group 99
Australian GP 18, 69, 70, 71, 132
Austrian GP 120, 121, 137, 142
Austro-Daimler car company 98
Autocar car company 94
Autodelta 85
Autódromo Hermanos Rodríguez 121
AutoJournal 24
Automobiles Alpine 106
Automobile Club de France (ACF) 9, 10
Automobile Club de la Sarthe 59
Automobile Club de l'Ouest 60
Automobile Club de Monaco 61
Automobile Club du Béarn 9
Automobiles Martini 53
Automobili Turismo e Sport (ATS) 51, 140
Auto Technisches Spezialzübehor (ATS) 99, 140
Auto Union 88, 94, 98
Avus 69, 97

B

Bad Homberg 10
Badoer, Luca 14, 52
Baghetti, Giancarlo 50
Baldi, Mauro 119
Balestre, Jean-Marie 23, 69
Ball, Micky 22
Bandini, Lorenzo 44, 122
Baracca, Count Enrico 35
Baracca, Francesco 34
Barnard, John 39, 104
Barrichello, Rubens 12, 15, 18, 37, 63, 123
Barzini, Luigi 67
Batista, Fulgencio 116
Battle of Britain 31
Battle of Calais 26
Battle of Crete 27
Baxter, Raymond 31
BBC 31
Beaujon, Michel 103
Behra, Jean 87, 145
Belgian GP 17, 51, 64, 70, 118
Bell, Derek 39, 44
Beltoise, Jean-Pierre 18, 63, 106
Benetton F1 team 14, 18, 39, 63, 64, 96, 101, 134, 141
Benoist, Robert 27
Benuzzi, Dario 37
Bérégovoy, Pierre 69
Berger, Gerhard 14, 18, 37, 49, 63, 132
Bernard, Eric 45, 105
Bernfeld, Ellen 139
Bernigaud, Jacqueline 69

Lightning Source UK Ltd.
Milton Keynes UK
UKHW01f1632170518
322764UK00001B/14/P

9 780955 486838